Praise for *Come Alive*

Yu Dan Shi's new book is full of insightful, evidence-based strategies and techniques that will help anyone live a happier and more fulfilled life. Coupled with a deeply personal narrative, this book is touching, engaging and emotive.

Professor Anthony Grant
Coaching Psychology, University of Sydney

When I read something that rattles me, and I keep coming back to it unintentionally well after I have put the book down, I know it's a good one! Reading Yu Dan's personal and confronting opening story about the Paradox of Success, I recognise clients and friends who also feel like they are winning on the outside but losing on the inside. In this powerful book, Yu Dan makes it clear that change is possible, and shows how it can be done. If you are questioning if there is more to life, this is a book that must be read ... And then actioned.

Corrinne Armour
Speaker, Trainer, Author 'Leaders Who Ask'

Yu Dan Shi skilfully combines ancient wisdom with modern evidence. She explores an important message about listening deeply to yourself before you design your future. Her skilful questions create a stirring inside you that will help you explore more and create a potent platform for a meaningful future.

Oscar Trimboli
Author 'Deep Listening'

Yu Dan's book *Come Alive* is exactly what the content will help you do. Yu Dan has successfully woven the science of positivity, meaning and a life well lived into a brave life story. It has been an absolute pleasure knowing Yu Dan and witnessing her strengths in action. I hope this "say it as it is" book will encourage more people to take the path Yu Dan has to make a positive difference in her own life and those whose lives she touches!

Dr Suzy Green
CEO & Founder, The Positive Institute

Sometimes the most profound truth comes from the simplest prose; stories that we can all relate to but habitually failed to see it for what they are. Yu Dan's clear and concise writing feels like it is my own voice coaching me on something I should have paid attention to long ago. *Come Alive* is an account of someone who have made it through a hollowing discovery and return to share with us the joy and passion that we can all unlock if we care to pay attention and take up the practice.

Chris Ho
Digital Transformation Leader, Photographer

There's a place in between the life you live and the life you want to live. This book takes you on a journey to close this gap. Yu Dan has nailed what it means to be ALIVE. This book breaks big concepts into easy to digest chunks that enables you to create change, meaning and joy now. There is no need to wait. As I read the book, tears rolled and it restored hope of what is possible and how we have the strength to come back from anything.

Dina Cooper
Creator of Parent as Leader, Author 'Smart Parenting'

Success does not equal happiness. But if you can find happiness, then you will surely be successful. Yu Dan's book is very timely with so many people examining themselves and questioning the path they are on. Yu Dan, through her own compelling personal story and drawing on research, shares how happiness and success are not exclusive. She also gives us a valuable guide on how to take control and find our own unique version of work and life balance.

Steven Norman
Founder of Growth Acumen, Author 'Future Proof Sales Strategy'

When I met Yu Dan I was unclear on my career, unsettled in my role and feeling like I was on a daily treadmill. I was tired and unsure of the changes I needed to make. I feel privileged to have met Yu Dan. She has been an inspiration to work with. Yu Dan has helped me be aware of my strengths, rethink work and life, and bring joy to what I do. I am now clearer on my career and how this fits with who I am. I have been able to redesign the life I want to live and now feel lighter and happier. Thank you Yu Dan.

Sema Musson
Culture & Organisation Transformation Leader

Working with Yu Dan has exceeded my wildest dreams. Yu Dan has incredible intuition, and this coupled with her amazing insights, experience and advice has resulted in the sessions being life-changing for me. Yu Dan is inspirational. She has taught me so much in a short period of time. I now carry these learnings with me and use them every day, in every aspect of my life. I feel lighter and happier as a person and more in control of my busy life. I really can't speak more highly of her and what she has to offer those that are lucky enough to meet her.

Jen Brown
Senior Director, CBRE

I approached Yu Dan when I was thinking to quit the investment bank industry because I was burned out, unhappy, and feeling lost. Since I started working with Yu Dan, I have completely changed within a short period of time. Yu Dan has unlocked my hidden strengths. I am happier, healthier, and feeling secure and confident about my life and career today. I still can't believe how much I have changed. It has been a truly amazing journey.

Wen Li
Technologist, Delivery Lead for Macquaire Bank,
Advisor for Digital Crew

Having been in the business for over 20 years, I've seen and worked with many coaches. Occasionally, you find a stand out one that delivers on exactly what they say. Yu Dan is one of those coaches. Her deep sense of passion and knowledge has proved invaluable. Her ability to quickly and succinctly get to the heart of the matter is both reassuring and powerful. Love working with Yu Dan.

Johnnie Cass
International Speaker, Trainer, Coach

When I met Yu Dan, I had encountered a career bottleneck and was unsure where to go. After entering into the coaching with Yu Dan, my life has changed completely. Yu Dan has helped me identify my strengths and clarify what I want to achieve in my life. Her practical guidance has led me to work on what I am passionate about within a short period of time. Now, I am clear with my direction to a happier and more meaningful life and career – it couldn't have happened without Yu Dan's help.

Cindy Tchung
Digital Marketing Executive, Meriton Group

Yu Dan, you have helped me change my life, and for the first time in many years, I am learning to use my strengths in many ways, every day and love myself again just as I am. Working with Yu Dan has helped me prioritise what is currently important in my life personally and professionally. Through our partnership, I feel stronger, re-focused, happier, and I feel like I am thriving again achieving greater results than I could have ever imagined.

Rachel Primrose
Leadership Consultant & Coach, Sage Consulting

come alive

Live a life with more meaning and joy

YU DAN SHI

First published in 2019 by Karen Mc Dermott Publishing, Perth, WA

Copyright ©2019 by Yu Dan Shi.

Come Alive: Live a Life with More Meaning and Joy. By Yu Dan Shi

1. Self-help. 2. Life skill. 3. Health & wellbeing. 4. Career development. 5. Success in business.

ISBN: 978-0-6485211-6-7 (paperback)
ISBN: 978-0-6485489-9-7 (eBook)

All rights reserved. No part of this publication may be reproduced, stored in a retrieval system, or transmitted in any form or by any means, electronic, mechanical, photocopying, recording, scanning, or otherwise, without the prior written permission of the author.

Front cover design by Lauren Shay
Proofread by Carolyn De Ridder

Printed in Australia

Disclaimer
This publication is designed to provide accurate and authoritative information in regard to the subject matter covered. While the publisher and author have used their best efforts in preparing this book, the material in this book is of the nature of general comment only. The advice contained herein may not be suitable for your situation. You should consult with a professional when appropriate. Neither the publisher nor the author shall be liable for any loss of profit or any other commercial damages, including but not limited to special, incidental, consequential, personal, or other damages.

For Jasmine, Angie, Mum, and Dad

CONTENTS

Introduction	11
Part I: The Paradox of Success	17
Chapter 1: Hollow Victory	19
Chapter 2: Stumbling on Happiness	33
Part II: A New Approach	49
Chapter 3: Living Well Today	51
Part III: Four Practices	69
Chapter 4: Care Less	71
Chapter 5: More Strength	92
Chapter 6: Do Less	115
Chapter 7: More Passion	134
Parting Words	*151*
Daily Practice Checklist	*153*
Next Steps	*155*
Acknowledgements	*156*
References	*158*
About the author	*169*

INTRODUCTION

One April afternoon in 2008, I was in a taxi on the way home after another day of business meetings. As the car was about to exit the Sydney Harbour Bridge, I suddenly felt very ill. I knew something was seriously wrong. I started to feel nauseous and excruciating pain on the right side of my body. I told the driver to take me to the nearest emergency room before I blacked out.

Thirty-six hours later, I was taken to an emergency operation. The doctor told me that my gallbladder was so infected it could rupture at any time. The condition was life-threatening if I left it any longer. I needed an operation immediately. It was a race against time.

My doctor also explained that I didn't have any reason to have this illness, given my age, weight and diet. I was only 32 years old. The only explanation was extreme stress.

As I sat there listening to the doctor describe my stress-related symptoms in disbelief, I was filled with remorse. The truth was, I was the cause of my pain and near-death experience.

I didn't need to ask the doctor how I had got there. I knew what my body was reacting to. It was the stress of looking successful on the outside and being completely miserable on the inside. I no longer had any passion for my job and had lost my drive and zest for life. I didn't know why and when I had started losing it, it was a perfect job in many ways.

I was a successful executive for a global technology company with a great salary. But I was miserable. I had struggled with this feeling for a long time, yet I had tried to fight it off by working insane hours and pretending everything was OK. For months, I had wanted to make a change but didn't do anything about it, fearing change would jeopardise my job, financial security and lifestyle. My illness was a result of my inaction, overwork and ongoing emotional battle.

I realised I had taken my life for granted. I had been given this precious thing called life, yet I had carelessly lived through it, always believing there would be tomorrow.

Sometimes, we don't have tomorrow.

For the first time in my life, I felt a deep sense of remorse. I regretted spending too much time on the things that didn't matter. I regretted not spending enough time with my family. I regretted not doing anything meaningful with my life.

When the doctor told me I urgently needed the operation, I was in intense pain, distress and shock. I didn't even have the mental clarity to explain what was happening to my family. I was too weak and terrified to tell anybody how severe it was. I was afraid saying the words out loud would make it too real; it would be a final goodbye. I didn't want to show anybody I was afraid but my heart ached as I hugged my kids, aged three and nine. I told everybody I would be fine, as I always did.

On the way to the operating room, my mind went blank except for one question: "Is this it?"

I asked God to give me one more chance, as there was so much I wanted to do, wanted to live for, and so many people I wanted to spend time with and love. I made a promise that if I came out alive from my operation, I would live my life very differently.

I survived the operation.

As painful and traumatic as it was, that day was the wake-up call I needed. I always thought I had a plan. My plan was to enjoy life after I had secured financial freedom, after I had made enough money, paid off my mortgage and sent my girls to university. On that fateful day, as I lay on the cold, hard gurney, I realised it was a very bad plan.

It was a safe plan I had been told my entire life, but it was a *big, fat* lie.

I decided I would find a way to live the way I wanted, every day, without waiting until the day I could afford it. Because you see, life doesn't work that way. Life can be snapped out of your hands in a split second.

To realise that and own that realisation was one of the biggest decisions I had ever made. But it was also the best decision I have ever made.

My moment of truth forced me to question the path I had pursued for so long: "Is it normal to never feel satisfied, even after achieving the pinnacle of success and career ambition? Or is something seriously wrong with me?"

Perhaps you have picked up this book because you're asking

yourself the same questions.

The truth was, I had an addiction to relentless ambition. My eyes were always on the next prize; what ever was bigger and better than the prize I had earned. I lived for tomorrow, an imaginative future of happiness and contentment that was always out of reach. I had convinced myself I was happy playing this perpetual game of chase. But the goals I chased weren't even mine to start with. Mostly, they were determined by others: my family, bosses, successful people I admired, and cultural and societal expectations.

I never asked myself the question, "Whose life am I living anyway?"

I needed the chasing game to end.

From that day, I started to change. It took many small changes and the breaking of many habits, but I found a new way to approach my work and life. I gave myself permission to be the person I was meant to be and found clarity, meaning and joy in my life.

I'm not going to lie: it was not easy to change. It was terrifying to imagine a different version of myself other than the highly-paid executive with a detailed plan and set of ambitious goals. It was hard to actively try to live with my true value.

I have had to learn to re-balance and re-focus my energy. I now invest less in the things that don't truly matter, the things that hold me back, and I focus more on the important, affirming and fulfilling things I need to thrive.

When you feel unfulfilled, miserable and stuck – maybe you're in the wrong job or the wrong profession – happiness can seem a million miles away. It's easy to imagine everything will be OK with a new project, a new job, a different career path or quitting altogether. You may have already experienced several career changes, only to feel empty and unfulfilled time and time again.

Most people find change terrifying, especially when it comes to their career. We have financial commitments and expectations, and we assume pursuing a new career or business requires sacrifice – we might need to let go of our secure income or start over completely. So, even when you are miserable, change doesn't seem like something to get excited about.

This book is not a career-transition guide. I have learned through my coaching practice that meaningful, long-lasting change only happens when we challenge and redefine our ideas about what success looks like. The blueprint for happiness isn't made with a cookie cutter, identical to the person next to us. We all have different strengths, passions and motivations. We are all energised in different ways and thrive in different environments. Learning how to tap into our best self and working towards lasting fulfilment are skills we need to develop and practice every single day.

This book will explain how you can transform the way you live and work, without the fear of radical change. You don't need to look outside yourself to change how you feel every day. You don't need to upend your life or quit everything to start over. You will start doing less of the things that steer you away from your vision and more of the things that bring it into sharp focus. You already have everything you need to start right now. This realisation will unlock a completely new energy source. You will come alive and be excited by the possibilities.

As the famous Chinese proverb goes: The journey of a thousand miles begins with a single step.

Are you ready to begin?

PART I

THE PARADOX OF SUCCESS

1
Hollow Victory

*If you work hard enough at it, you can grind
even an iron rod down to a needle.*
CHINESE PROVERB

Remember the adage, "You can be anything if you put your mind to it?"

For me, this wasn't just a saying. This was my core belief, which I held onto every day of my life. Work hard, study hard and you will achieve greatness. Guaranteed.

As a child growing up in a poor village in China, working and studying hard was more than a pathway to becoming anything I wanted. It was my only means of escaping the poverty and hardship I experienced every day.

I embarked on my ambitious journey at a very young age. I

started school at the age of four. When most children were playing with mud in my village, I was buried in textbooks. But my hard work was rewarded. At just eight years of age, I was accepted into high school. You might think I was a child prodigy. I was bright, sure. But I also wanted to grow up quickly so I could provide for my family. I desperately wanted to alleviate the financial pain my mum went through every day, and desperation can push you to do anything. I never slowed down and was always learning on a rapid and steep curve.

I graduated from university when I was 17. I started my corporate career in Shanghai, then moved to Sydney to study my MBA at age 21. I came to Australia with two suitcases and a winter coat stuffed with dry food to save money. Like many immigrants, I found adapting to a new country a long and difficult road. I studied my MBA full time while working as a waitress at night.

Once I secured a job in Australia, my progress continued rapidly. Then, at the aged of 31, I became a Chief Marketing Officer for the Australian arm of a global tech company. To me, it was more than a job. It was an immigrant dream come true. But that was really no surprise to me – after all, if you worked hard, you could be anything. I had proven this core belief of mine to be true.

I never questioned the path I was on until one day when a defining moment changed the direction of my life. At the time, I didn't know how it would change or where it would lead, but I remember that day so clearly.

The paradox of success: Winning on the outside, losing on the inside

It was the spring of 2007. My office had a spectacular view over Sydney Harbour. It was simply breathtaking. It was the perfect postcard image, one I had seen as a young girl living in China. In fact, it had inspired me as a wide-eyed 21-year old to leave my life and family behind in Shanghai, filled with hope that this city would be the beginning of a new adventure and a better life.

Imagine me, a young Chinese migrant, the daughter of poor academics, born in a remote village in China, 10 years later having an executive role in a leading Fortune 100 technology company, with a view of one of the most iconic harbours in the world from my desk? It was as if a Hollywood script-writer had written my story.

That day, I turned away from my mountain of work to look at the view. Like every other day, the harbour glittered magnificently and white sailing boats glided through the water. As I looked at the harbour, a strange feeling came over me. It was a feeling completely foreign to me, a void, a sense of emptiness.

There I was, trapped in a boxed office, poring over endless spreadsheets and charts, enduring mind-numbing boardroom meetings, discussing things I didn't even care about, while that world-famous harbour was right there in front of me. I wanted to walk in the sun and enjoy the beautiful day outside, but I was trapped, as I was every day, with endless work, not knowing when it would end.

This feeling hit me by complete surprise. I'd had many ups and downs in my life, many struggles and hardships, but I'd always had a fire in my belly. I had always been full of zest, energy and action, forever on the go and excited about opportunities and possibilities. Life felt full. I felt full. Yet, as I sat in my office overlooking the dazzling Sydney Harbour, I felt lost and empty.

For as long as I remembered, I always had a clear direction. I'd always been a goal-setter and had written my annual plan religiously since the age of 15. I never get lost. How could you feel lost when all your visions and plans were beautifully mapped out and reviewed every year?

On the surface, I had everything. I was the opposite of empty. As an executive of an innovative global tech company, I had a great job with a salary to match. I had ticked every life-goal box: a family with two beautiful children, houses and lovely cars. I was told this was success and happiness. So why, after all these years of hard work and success, did I feel this way?

The feeling persisted. It was suffocating. I had always been so positive and passionate. What had happened? I felt burdened and stressed. The work was sucking the energy out of me.

For the first time ever, I didn't have the energy to face my work. I knew I had been pretending to love my work and inspire my team. But how could I inspire anyone when I didn't want to be there? I felt like a fraud.

Suddenly, everything around me in the office felt like a circus. I was putting on a show. I smiled at people all day long, put my best foot forward. I was hard-working and dedicated. It was easy to fake it.

I had the urge to walk out of the office, into the sun and be free. "I can't do this anymore. I will quit my job and find a job I will be passionate about." I swore to myself.

Looking around me, everybody was in the thick of action,

oblivious to what was going through my mind. There were piles of documents to be reviewed, emails to be replied to and reports to be generated. All this needed to be done by 5pm before I rushed out the door to beat the traffic and pick up my daughters from school and daycare.

On the way home, reality sank in. "I can't just walk out of a job without a plan," I told myself, "I have a family to support."

What was I going to do anyway? Corporate marketing in the technology sector was all I knew. Starting again was totally impractical. I had a family to support and a mortgage to pay. It had taken me 15 years to be where I was, I couldn't afford to invest another 15 years into pursuing a different path. I didn't have the time nor the energy. I couldn't pursue my happiness at the cost of my children's future.

That evening, after I put my kids to bed, I sat down in my study to try to catch up with my mountain of work. But I struggled to stay focused. My thoughts went back to what had happened that afternoon.

"I shouldn't be feeling this way," I thought. "How dare I feel this way, even for a moment?" Everything I had was a world away from my impoverished childhood. I had worked hard for so long to get to that point. The last thing I wanted was to feel hopelessly lost. I should have felt the opposite – utterly and eternally grateful.

Fear of failure and being a "disappointment"

Noble goals and actions, such as striving for success and financial security, are often driven by internal fears.

Life in China was difficult when I was growing up. I was the child of two parents who both went through the Cultural Revolution.

At 18 years of age, shortly after being accepted into university, my parents had to leave their home and live on remote farms for 10 years, in the prime of their lives. Instead of pursuing their dreams of study and careers, they worked as hard labourers, lived in shelters and could not visit their families. Those 10 years were tragic. The darkness, the loneliness and the emotional pain they had to endure were immense.

Many people from that generation did not survive the ordeal. The survivors, like my parents, carried their psychological scars with them for the rest of their lives. The next generation of children, including my brother and I, suffered greatly because of that. As our parents' dreams had been lost, we became their only hope.

What my parents went through altered the course of their lives. Their unfulfilled hopes and dreams were inevitably projected onto me, their eldest child. They wanted a better life for me, a young girl with my future stretched out before me. I knew my parents made a lot of sacrifices for me. I always felt I owed them a debt of gratitude for whatever opportunities I was given and I could never fail to meet their high expectations. This was a huge burden to carry and I never realised how profoundly it would influence my life.

My childhood was underscored by constant anxiety about our family's financial situation. We spent many years apart. My father studied in Shanghai, 200 kilometres outside our hometown, Chongming Island, in the hope of getting a degree and a better job to support us. There was no money for travelling expenses, so I only saw my father twice a year during the first few years of my life. My mother had no choice but to give up her dream of going to university to take care of my brother and me.

I grew up in a mud house with brick walls over a mud floor. It was always wet and dark, especially in the winter or rainy weather. There were no electric lights and no windows. We had a bed, a table, some stools and a chest of drawers. My brother and I studied under an oil lamp. The light was so dim, we couldn't study for long and would go to bed before 7pm as it hurt our eyes.

At the age of four, I had to walk to school by myself in icy-cold winters. My ears and fingers felt frozen, but I never felt defeated. I would hold my little head high, walking into the wind, not allowing myself to cry. The more pain I felt on those icy mornings, the more determined I became that my future would change for the better.

I watched my mother get up at 4am every day and spend hours just to make a thin porridge, coughing as the smoke from the big, black oven filled her lungs. Every day, I watched her count every cent we had and I would hear her cry in the middle of the night, worrying about our future. I wanted to help but I was just a child. I dreamt about buying a big house for my parents so they would never have to worry again. In fact, when I was nine years old, I told them that was my plan. I swore that one day, we would live in a place so safe and secure, nobody would cry over money or worry about the future again.

Then, my mother started to struggle to raise us financially. She was forced to make a very difficult decision and sent my brother away for several years. It wasn't safe for a girl to be away from her parents, so I stayed with my mother. To survive, my family was broken and separated. It took 12 years for us to finally reunite and move to Shanghai after my father eventually got his lecturer post at a university after he solved a significant mathematical equation.

As the eldest child, I carried most of the burden to fulfil my parents' lost dreams. I tried my best to reach whatever heights I could to make my mum happy. I couldn't wait to grow up so I could make everything right, so I could make all those dreams happen.

What's your anchor?

There are many anchors that hold us back in life. It's hard to see how deep they go when we are in the thick of it. To be free, we need to let go of these traps. Being aware of what our anchors are is the first step. Financial security has been my biggest anchor and has heavily influenced all my life decisions.

I never worked for status. I worked because I wanted to provide a better future for my family and myself.

I remember when I was 15 years old, I told my parents I wanted to be a writer. It created such tension in my family. My father, a mathematician, gave me all the facts and reasons why this was such a bad idea. I would be a poor artist living on the streets. Most writers could barely make a living; it was an unsafe route. I quickly forgot about my silly dream of writing. Instead, I studied computer science, a safe choice with job security and career potential. I hear the same stories from my clients all the time no matter which culture they were born.

Even if you don't share my upbringing, you can probably relate to this.

Abraham Maslow described the motivation for safety and security in his *hierarchy of needs theory*. As humans, Maslow explained, our motivations are focused on our basic need to survive first. Then, as this need is met, our motivations turn to the next level in a hierarchy, from safety, belonging and love, to esteem and self-actualisation.

Achieving a state of financial security is the primary concern of many of the people I meet and work with. It consumes us. However, instead of moving up the hierarchy, we tend to get stuck at this lower level of the hierarchy of needs because greed, debt and status drive us to focus on earning more, having more, and being more in order to feel safe.

We start this habit young, during our school years, when instead of learning for joy and personal growth, we learn how to graduate with good marks. We are more concerned that our education leads us to bigger and better things, rather than appreciating the knowledge we gain or the passion we discover along the way.

When we apply the same principle in adulthood, life becomes a game of chess: each move is a stepping stone to get us to a stronger position. Unfortunately, for most of us, no stepping stone is ever enough to make us feel secure. We want more material wealth, so we take on more debt. We work even harder to get a rise in salary and position, hoping one day life will be easier – when the mortgage is more manageable or when the kids leave school and there are no more school fees. We work harder and harder, always imagining a future where we don't have to work anymore.

First taste of freedom

Having a computer science degree and above-average English skills was a killer combination in 1993. Foreign companies had just started to flood into China, especially Shanghai. I was among the first generation of people in China who could choose to work for private foreign corporations. As a country, we had never had so much freedom and opportunity before.

Once I graduated from university at 17, I wanted to succeed in my first job. I would regularly work from 8am until midnight. I was efficient, fast and did more work than people much older than me. I worked every day. I was promoted and the opportunities kept coming my way, so I just kept going.

Every time I got a pay rise or another promotion, I worked even harder. I saw working hard as the path to financial freedom. My first month's salary was four times what my father earned as a university professor and renowned mathematician. By the time I was 18, I was earning US$500 a month. At that point, I was earning more in a month than my father earned in an entire year.

The financial reward completely blindsided me. I forgot about my aspiration to be a writer. Just 10 years earlier, we were still relying on my mother's monthly salary of US$5 for a family of four. I suddenly realised I was on a route to massive financial reward and success.

I could afford to buy things for myself as well as my parents. I wanted to spoil them so badly. We never went to restaraunts when I was young. When I was 19 years old, I took my parents on a holiday to China's capital city, Beijing. We went to nice restaurants and stayed in a five-star hotel. I could see the tears in my mum's eyes. They were so proud of me, and I wanted to make them happy.

I climbed the corporate ladder for another 15 years, confident my success would bring happiness to my entire family. I had no doubt that if I just kept going, I would soon reach my life's goal of complete security. I would achieve my dream of escaping poverty and building a prosperous life for myself and my family – not just for my daughters, but my parents, too. I would not disappoint them. All the sacrifices they had made during those years of hardship would have been worthwhile. I wanted to ensure all their hopes and dreams had not been wasted on me.

Feeling stuck with no way out

I had worked tirelessly to get to that point in my career while raising a family, pulling endless late nights, midnight conference calls, all to prove myself worthy.

Yet there I was, at the height of my career, and I could no longer keep going. I no longer *wanted* to keep going. I was afraid to ask an even deeper, more profound question do I even want this anymore?

Despite my generous income, the cost of living in Australia was high and I couldn't fulfil my promise. I had promised my parents I would buy them a house one day and bring them to Australia, but this hadn't happened. The guilt consumed me every day. I felt like I had let my parents and myself down.

And what about my girls? If I didn't continue this corporate path with the same level of income, how could I provide for them? What if I made a bad decision and lost everything through my stupidity? I had worked so hard to give my girls everything I didn't have as a child. Now I no longer wanted to continue this path, I felt I had failed not only as a person but also as a mother and a daughter. I felt weak and selfish.

I also had another dilemma. I realised I knew nothing about myself. I had no idea what my real talent was. Despite the fact I was a Chief Marketing Officer for a technology company and had previously run business units across dozens of countries, I didn't feel I had any talents I could use outside the corporate tech world.

Chasing my elusive pot of gold

I thought I had followed the right path, a path that would lead me to success and a bright future. I always thought I would be happy once I got there. I had spent my entire career focusing on getting there. My eyes were forever on the next role and the one after next, up the corporate ladder. I never questioned where I was headed.

I had been running so fast and was so sure all my hard work would pay dividends. I bet my entire career to win this prize – a place where I no longer felt poor, unsafe, worthless and weak. I was so sure my life in Australia, a world away from my upbringing in China, would make me feel safe, strong and happy.

I had been searching for the pot of gold at the end of the rainbow and discovered it was an illusion. To travel so far and end up completely lost was devastating. Dr Tony Grant, my professor and a coaching psychologist at the University of Sydney, calls this a "Hollow Victory".

The patterns and habits that lead us to where we are

If you have lost your passion and motivation after years of hard work, it didn't happen overnight. I believe that what we experience today is often the result of a short-term strategy that has become a long-term, destructive pattern. Our tactics to succeed may have worked once and given us a professional boost, but over time these patterns can sabotage our happiness.

These detrimental habits and patterns are things like working tirelessly at the expense of sleep, relationships, well-being and life balance; saying "yes" to everything to show how committed we are then pushing ourselves to the ground to manage an ever-expanding workload; striving for perfectionism; prioritizing other people's goals over our own.

These habits are often rewarded by organisations and society. We quickly discover they help us get ahead, so we keep doing them, even when they don't make us happy. When these strategies become a daily habit, they inevitably wear us down, no matter how successful we are in our career.

My original intent behind pursuing a successful corporate career was a good one: I wanted to help my family and live a better life. Being driven to achieve goals was a good trait. However, I let my career ambition and the endless chasing of goals overtake many important areas in my life. I worked 14 hours a day, working a second shift after putting my kids to bed and turning up for conference calls with my global team at 1am just to name a few. I also stopped myself from pursuing the things I really enjoyed in life out of concern they would make me less driven.

Before my diagnosis, as I grappled with my dilemma, I started to experience regular sharp pains on the right side of my body, so bad that on some nights I had to lie on the cold, hard floor, clutching my stomach in agony, as that was the only way to alleviate my pain. But I kept working, trying to block out the pain. I thought it might just be another stomach ulcer episode and hoped it would go away eventually. I continued to turn up to work with a happy and strong façade. I kept telling myself, "Don't be a quitter. You have had it good, don't rock the boat. Be grateful, go back to work and stay focused. There is no time for this self-pity."

Little do we realise that if we keep operating this way, our success will be short-lived. Humans can't go far without sustained motivation. We thrive on positive energy and experiences. Like a fuel tank, our energy must be replenished daily. In my case, my stubbornness to persevere and stay tough brought me success in my career but almost cost me my life. I was rapidly running out of steam.

To turn the situation around so we can thrive, not just survive, we need to fundamentally shift the way we work and live. We need to rethink our priorities and where we focus our energy. We need to take a step back and re-examine our beliefs and working habits. Understanding the paradox of success is a crucial step.

Reflection

- What long-term beliefs have made you successful at work but caused you unhappiness in your life?

2
Stumbling on Happiness

Happiness is the meaning and the purpose of life, the whole aim and end of human existence.
ARISTOTLE

How many of us hope, "If I can achieve this, I will be happier." Yet constantly feel unfulfilled?

Having a progress mindset is important but the time, energy and effort we devote to our goals need be focused in the right direction. Too often, we choose the wrong direction.

My story was straight from a film script – a real-life rags-to-riches plotline. From struggling to survive an impoverished childhood, I overcame adversity to succeed in a foreign country.

Except I didn't feel like the hero of the story. I felt like a fraud.

It was a huge shock to realise I was so unhappy after achieving my hard-fought goal. But it was inevitable. Trading your happiness and health today for a reward in the future is ultimately futile for many people.

Hopefully, you don't have to experience a traumatic medical emergency like I did to realise that stress and unhappiness rarely lead to joy and freedom. Mostly, it leads to more stress and more unhappiness.

Stumbling on happiness

I sat down one day and wrote a list of all the things I strived for. I realised that I measured my success by how much I could impress others and make people proud. My own happiness was not on that list; it didn't matter. Realising that was a real eye-opener. For the first time in my life, I understood I didn't even know what would make me happy.

I started researching happiness in early 2009. This felt silly at the time. I was sceptical about topics such as happiness; I was logical and grounded, whereas happiness felt like something airy-fairy. But clearly, whatever I had done so far was not giving me happiness.

I came across the "Happiness & Its Causes" conference during my research, and it just so happened it would be held in Sydney that year. I was astonished there was a conference about happiness. I wasn't sure whether I should attend. Should I wear a love-heart t-shirt? Should I buy a "happy" notebook? What if people saw me?

Curiosity got better of me. I went to the conference. There were, indeed, quite a few people wearing their happy t-shirts, but most were just like me, seemingly logical and normal.

On that day, a moment changed my life for the better. When Dr Suzy Green, an Australian positive psychologist, walked on to the stage to present her talk on hope, she absolutely radiated. Something about her presence touched my heart deeply. I could feel something I was not used to feeling: *joy*. It was the same feeling I had when I looked at my kids or when I was in love, but rarely outside these situations.

I realized the happiness I usually felt was different from the joy Dr Green experienced. Her joy came from her heart, from herself, right at that moment. My occasional happiness almost always came as a form of reward, from outside, after something I had achieved.

This is the difference between pleasure and happiness.

Pleasure is fleeting because it comes from external sources. Happiness is renewable because it comes from within.

When we only focus on the pleasure of external goals, it creates a void that can never be filled. We can acquire more things or more accolades, but they only serve temporary needs. Like an addiction, the only way to feel happy again is to acquire more. If we keep trying to fill our void with external pleasures, one day, we will question why the emptiness continues to return.

I realised I had been valuing the external thrill far more than my inner joy, and this was the reason why I stayed in my job. As long as I was in my job, I fit into society's definition of success. For a long time, I was willing to trade my happiness for that, until the thrill stopped working its magic.

The myth that ambition leads to happiness

We have been conditioned to believe success is the same for everyone. The "ambition condition" instills the idea that we need to have ambition and drive to feel fulfilled. However, we are given a very narrow definition of what ambition and drive look like (or is socially acceptable).

We have been indoctrinated to think of success in absolute terms – big salary, status, career, beauty, awards, expensive possessions, the perfect family, being popular.

Why don't we consider ourselves successful when we have great relationships? Or when we have time for the things we value? Or when we live our life truthfully?

How many of us choose our careers, where we live, what schools we send our children to, the car we drive, who we marry and so on based on society's definition of success, even at the cost of our happiness and freedom? How many people live in quiet desperation, hopeful that by making sensible, safe choices, contentment will follow?

This idea of success has become entrenched in our subconscious. When we meet someone, we often ask, "What do you do? Where do you live?" How often do we ask, "Are you happy? Are you fulfilled?"

The purpose of every day is to check things off the grocery list of life. Good education – tick. Good job – tick. Better job with more money – tick. Loving life partner, fancy house and kids – tick, tick, tick (bonus points for having them in that order). Life is good.

Then the goal posts move and we strive for even more items on the checklist: big promotion to a senior-level management position, higher salary with a bonus, fancier house, fancier car, investment portfolio, private-school education for the kids, holiday house. And when you check off everything on the list, you can finally say: "I have it all."

But "having it all" rarely happens. It's a mirage. We think we can see it in the distance, but it vanishes when we arrive. We always want more.

Now, imagine the items on the checklist were replaced with "joy", "growth" and "freedom". How many boxes could you tick?

Of course, you need money to eat and have a roof over your head. But once you have these things, wealth and status are merely external symbols of success. A research conducted by economist Angus Deaton and noble prize winning psychologist Daniel Kahneman over 450,000 people found our emotional wellbeing doesn't improve as wealth increases after US$75,000 income threshold.

People with "good jobs" often put creative dreams and life-long passions on hold for fear of jeopardising their social status, bank balance and plans for a renovation or overseas holiday. You may have a fancy title, a great salary, and an impressive resume, but they only look good on paper.

The social construct of success drives us to value things that might lead us to the wrong path. I was always focused on external growth. To me, success meant constantly moving upwards. I saw every step up as proof I was succeeding. In truth, I was continuously moving in the wrong direction. I was no longer growing internally and had reached stagnation. In other words, by continuing the trajectory I was on, I was limiting my true potential. No matter how much more money and status I achieved, if I was not growing and thriving, I was one of the walking dead.

We adopt beliefs, values and follow the playbook written by others without honouring our innermost feelings and true purpose. These easy-to-follow scripts might have given us the taste of initial success and achievement. However, blindly following them without ever checking our internal compass creates enormous disconnection.

The dream you chase, is it really yours? I know mine wasn't. It was one of my parents', society's, far away from what I initially wanted. But I believed my dream was less ambitious, less driven and less certain compared with the social standard.

Are you hoping happiness will arrive one day?

For most of my life, I believed happiness was the result of hard work. Like death and taxes, the need to struggle in order to succeed and be happy was one of life's only certainties. A well-paid job should be mentally taxing, hard, boring, uninspiring – otherwise, it wouldn't be called work. People who are good at their jobs don't slack off and enjoy themselves. They have goals, ambitions. Just like the hero's story, no matter how difficult the journey, I pictured myself succeeding despite the odds and I chased that image of myself relentlessly.

As a young girl in China, whenever I was tired and complained about how hard my study was, my mum and teachers would say, "There are only a few more years to go before you finish school and go to university, then your life will be set." So, I thought I only had to persist for a few more years, then the pain would be gone and I would live happily ever after. This voice in my head kept telling me, "I will be happy soon, it's just around the next corner."

Most of us believe that to be successful, pain is inevitable. We keep pushing ourselves, even though we know we're not enjoying our everyday work lives. We convince ourselves it is a worthwhile price to pay; one day, we will be where we want to be and we can enjoy ourselves. If you are a coporate warrior like I was for 20+ years, you would know that our life consists of many grueling days with fleeting happy moments. I can't say I know many professionals who enjoy their days and are happy. We have even accepted this to be the norm, a way of life until we can afford to retire.

When we were children, we could easily enjoy ourselves. Somewhere along the way, we lost the ability to enjoy life. We might still enjoy a nice glass of wine, our morning coffee or a beautiful holiday. But these are rare moments. Most of the time, we work, we get through life and we try to keep up.

I never stopped to ask: "Is this what I really want?" It sounds silly. You might not be happy now but you will be happy eventually, right? Isn't that what it's all about? Isn't that why we work so hard, so we can get somewhere someday and be happy? Why would we make all these sacrifices otherwise?

Chasing strips away our natural ability to enjoy life

When I was going through my journey, I realised that most of my unhappiness came from my addiction to future rewards. I needed the thrill of the chase. I could always find something bigger around the corner and it was exhilarating to work towards these goals. Like a mountain climber, as I reached one summit, I would see another mountain in the distance, even higher and more challenging.

I was never satisfied.

Focusing on tomorrow's summit overshadowed my natural ability to enjoy where I was today. I didn't take in the view and enjoy what I already had.

But life isn't a series of Mount Everest climbs and Hollywood fairy tales. In chasing these dramatic successes, we forget the true meaning of life, the simplicity and joy that already exist in our day-to-day work and life, the opportunities to do more and help more. Instead, we bet on these gigantic moments of ecstasy to deliver us the ultimate happiness.

There is nothing wrong with pursuing worthwhile goals and aspirations. The problem is when we feel endless need, greed and desire. No matter how much you achieve, it never feels enough. When our ability to enjoy today gets replaced by chasing endless goals, it's very difficult to stay happy. Over time, you are bound to ask what is happening. If you are not happy today, it's unlikely you will be happy tomorrow.

Although I chose a corporate career over being a writer, my jobs were good. For a long time, I was passionate about my career, as it gave me the intellectual stimulation and learning I needed. However, over time, parts of the jobs I had no longer aligned with my values and talents. Instead of taking time to reflect on this and find better ways to work, I pushed myself to try harder and used the dangling carrots of promotion, bonuses and social recognition to stay artificially motivated.

I went from being passionate about my career to being passionate about the rewards that came with it. That tactic worked for a while.

But once the rewards stopped working, I felt completely disconnected from my job – in fact, from my entire life, as everything had centred around the prizes and rewards I received. All my joy and self-worth disappeared as well.

I realised I was not unhappy. I simply had never allowed myself to be happy until I had got to another destination, until I had ticked another box. I didn't feel that I deserved to be happy until I had reached my final destination, wherever that was.

Over time, I no longer knew how to experience joy.

We need daily motivation to keep going

I believe what underpins this behaviour is that we don't know how to achieve success in a healthy way. We have been taught a very narrow version of how to live successfully. Most of us believe putting happiness on hold is the price we pay to achieve success. We believe that to be successful, we must put ourselves through endless rounds of misery. Only after we have overcome every challenge presented to us can we declare we are happy.

We have been conditioned to stay motivated by the prize at the end. We forget that we need energy and motivation daily to keep us going. If you drain your daily energy, you have nothing left. You either burn out and quit before you reach the end, which makes you feel bad about yourself, or you earn the prize but with resentment and no energy to enjoy it. Doing it all over again requires all your willpower.

The easier way to achieve your goals is to feel motivated and energised daily. This allows your body to recover naturally, so you don't need to draw on supreme willpower all the time. We all have a limited supply of willpower and energy to draw from. Protecting your energy is vital to sustained success.

If you spend lots of time artificially motivating yourself, it will take a toll on your mental, physical and psychological wellbeing, eventually, we could stop achieving altogether as we couldn't keep going anymore. So, the key is to always ask yourself, "Does this give me enough motivation now as well as into the future? Or am I just eyeing the prize and putting myself into another round of misery?"

People often say, "I had always been driven, what has happened to me? I thought I would be happier now but actually, I was happier when I started out in my career when I had less money and status." External rewards can only sustain us for so long. Eventually, they wear off. You may feel you are no longer driven but it is more likely you have been driven by the wrong goals. Your motivation will return once you set goals and priorities that are meaningful to you.

Understanding our inner most motivation

Our soul can only be nourished through natural motivation. Working only for external rewards and ignoring our inner needs makes us miserable.

Fundamentally, our understanding of how motivation works is wrong. The way we are motivated and rewarded incentivises the wrong behaviours and habits. Money, status, promotions and recognition for our workaholic ambitions – these external incentives encourage us to pursue even more external rewards, instead of making time for the things that matter most to us.

For instance, as a small child, I loved learning. When I realised education could give me another reward – skipping grades, feeling worthy of my parents' love and sacrifice – I stopped learning for the joy of it. I started treating education as a means to an end. I studied to get somewhere, to prove I was good enough, to hide my insecurity and pain.

Most people learn at a young age that praise and awards from teachers and parents are prizes worth receiving. Not many of us have been encouraged to do things simply because we enjoy them. Teaching children to seek external validation deprives them of the opportunity to value and embrace their own source of joy. We repeat the same pattern as adults, never understanding how destructive this is.

Yet the things we choose to do without the promise of any external reward or validation are often the things we love the most. It's also when we perform our best. Think about how parents love their children unconditionally without any reward.

It doesn't mean we shouldn't enjoy external rewards but striving for them alone takes us away from our true purpose and focus in life. Internal drive is a more natural way of feeling motivated; it gives us more joy and satisfaction.

If we learn how to listen to our own motivation, we will learn how to choose the right path, the right projects. Every time we are faced with a decision, we will have a clear process of choosing what is right for us. We will be able to say yes and no easily. We will start to experience more of "we want to" moments instead of "we have to" moments. Every morning, we can get out of the bed genuinely looking forward to the day ahead.

Developmental Psychology

Our desire to create a life that is more aligned with our internal motivation is a natural developmental process. I didn't realise it at the time, but my feelings of emptiness were messages from my true self. The void I felt was a calling. If you learn to identify these defining moments and are open to the lessons they teach, you can re-direct yourself and make better choices.

One of my deepest fears at the time was the fear of failure. What if pursuing a different path meant going backwards and I could never replicate the same level of success? I feared losing my sense of security and financial freedom. It would be a humiliating fall from grace. The thought of going backwards financially brought all my insecurities about poverty to the surface.

Each time I looked for a logical, sensible and well-worn path, I always came back to where I already was. It seemed like the safest path and fear told me to stop jeopardising it. At the time, the fear was overwhelming and it felt like I was making a life-or-death decision.

In reality, I was experiencing a completely normal stage of life – part of the developmental pattern. Research has long shown that as we reach a certain life stage starting from our 30s, we start to think about the limited time we have left. This inflection point usually occurs 10-15 years into your career.

This is the point at which our sense of urgency to find meaning and purpose kicks in. Especially in your mid-30 and 40s, these personal needs and conflicting priorities become more apparent. We feel an urgency to reconcile ourselves with whatever uncertainty or lost dreams we have had. Our need to resolve these issues becomes more pressing. It's important to know we are not having a crisis. Wanting more meaning, purpose and joy in your life is absolutely normal. It's part of a more complete human experience. It's OK to become more reflective as we grow older. We want a life well-lived and we want growth and connection with the things we value.

I wish I had seen this pivotal time in my life as a signpost pointing me in a new direction rather than a breaking point. Because really, how I felt was normal. As we get older, our priorities change. Human beings always gravitate towards new growth and if we feel stagnant, we need to find a way to break the inertia.

At each turning point, we should listen to our inner thoughts and embrace the opportunity to grow. To change the things that aren't working, we need to be open to new possibilities and commit ourselves to self-discovery and growth. Positive change will only happen when we embrace our goals willingly.

Pay attention to the defining moments

Defining moments are everywhere. One of the tendencies we have when we face setbacks in life is we rush through the process trying to find an answer; we don't pause enough to reflect and listen to our inner voice. In fact, we often shut down these voices so we don't have to face the truth.

For me, instead of working through these emotions, I tried to block my feeling by working harder, indulging myself with retail shopping, holidays, and pretending to be positive and grateful. All the tactics only gave me temporary relief and prevented me from being honest with myself. But the internal struggle never went away, it built up so much that eventually led me to my illness, but my emotion was so blocked that I couldn't even tell how severe my physical pain was until it became life-threatening.

I thought it was a great trait by showing up as a strong person despite my inner conflict; this same ability has helped me achieve in spite of a difficult upbringing. I now realise that was my safe way of masking pain and unease. I was confusing toughness with real courage. When we cover every adversity and sadness with appearing tough, when this becomes our only operating mode, we lose the ability to acknowledge what was happening objectively. We close ourselves off: not only we have robbed ourselves of being in touch of our feelings, we have also robbed ourselves opportunity to explore things more deeply and come up with better ways.

The sooner we respond to this mental conflict, the more satisfied we will be in life and at work. Studies show that people who have managed these turning points successfully can grow a new sense of self-awareness and a higher-level of harmony and satisfaction.

If you don't take the time to understand yourself, what truly drives you, how you work at your best, it doesn't matter whether you have the best job in the world or set up your own business. Your pattern will repeat again and again. Over time, it will likely cost you your health, relationships and, ultimately, your happiness.

Without this simple shift in the way we work and live, we are at risk of constant dissatisfaction even after we are in our "dream job or business". It is not uncommon for people who are successfully doing what they love to do lose their passion and no longer enjoy it. Passion is important but our daily habits can make or break us.

Creating a satisfying life is *a skill* we need to master, not something that will magically happen just because you think you have earned it.

When you understand you can change your situation, and when you understand how you can change it, you will feel confident and in control of your own path. I often see clients who have wrestled with lost motivation and emptiness for years feeling the fire in their belly again within a short period of time. The drive was always there but they needed the right set of priorities to bring their motivation back. Be kind to yourself. Allow yourself time and space to reflect and embrace new priorities in your life.

In Chapter 3, we will explore how you can start to make positive and meaningful changes.

....

Reflection

- What defining moments have you encountered?
- What did they teach you?

....

PART II

A NEW APPROACH

3
Living Well Today

Success is liking yourself, liking what you do, and liking how you do it.
MAYA ANGELOU

Many people shy away from changing the course of their lives because it seems too hard. However, with the right knowledge, you can navigate change successfully. When managed effectively, change can be exciting and empowering. On the other hand, remaining stuck is painful and self-limiting.

When I first started my journey, I had to read how to manage fear to calm myself down. Our culture says that to create change, you must be brave and take the jump. But even the bravest people take a calculated risk. You need more than pure courage and bravery to enact change. You also need effective strategies to help you navigate the change.

Many people deal with change in a drastic manner. They believe they must let go of the past completely and start anew. This sounds scary and overwhelming, so they end up doing nothing.

This is because often, people *confuse* the result of change with the process of change.

From the moment I wanted to make a change to ending up on the operating table one year later fighting for my life, I had made almost no attempt to improve my situation. I read books and searched the Internet for answers, but I never did anything about it. I woke up every day with the same mindset, same habits and same behaviour. Yet there I was, hoping one day my life would be brilliant and significantly different from today.

I thought change was a life-or-death decision. I thought I had to choose one path or the other, right there and then. The emotions I went through were unbearable. Deep down, I didn't know how to make effective changes.

Change doesn't have to be daunting. You don't have to turn your life upside down and throw away everything you have achieved.

Change is a gradual process

We don't need to change everything to be happier, what we need is small adjustments and refinement. As James Clear observes in his book *Atomic Habits*, you only need 1% of improvement every day to achieve great results.

Many people at this juncture spend a lot of time searching for their purpose or that "one perfect thing". They might travel the world, visit somewhere remote or attend lots of workshops. I have done a couple of these things myself.

The problem with this approach is that you might be able to find a moment of clarity when there are no distractions, but this clarity is forgotten once you return to your normal life because your habits and mindset haven't changed.

I have discovered a simpler way – and that is, through learning to connect with your natural needs daily, you naturally discover and live with your purpose, fulfilment and joy. Through regular action and observation, you will notice what motivates you, what brings you joy and what has held you back.

Instead of making drastic changes, you learn to improve your current situation while bringing in new experiences and habits over time. This gradual process gives you the opportunity to reflect on what has got in the way and what adjustments you need to make to create a more satisfying life.

Instead of spending years hoping for a perfect moment of clarity, you learn to discover your clarity through daily actions and experimentation.

Why? Because that's the easiest way to get started. Once we create action, it creates motion, energy and momentum and it becomes an ongoing cycle. Inaction says, "I can't." Action says, "I can." Imperfect action always exceeds perfect inaction.

This is the art of change: our actions drive our mindset change. London Business School professor Herminia Ibarra has observed that when we think then act, we tend to act under the same problematic mindset. But when we start acting first, our behaviour changes our thinking.

To make change work, we need to make change easy; one change at a time, one habit at a time.

Your external situation is only half the equation

When I first started my journey, I spent a lot of time thinking about a future solution. I counted on finding my future happiness in another job, another career, living in a coastal town, writing my books, anything I could think of that could get me out of there. I thought my job was my only source of unhappiness. I spent all my energy searching for an alternative. I failed to see my role in the problem that I was the co-contributor to my situation.

I thought I was striving for a higher goal but in truth, I wasn't running towards anything at all. I was running away to avoid facing the truth. Psychologists call this the "avoidance goal".

I also blamed my situation on others and circumstance –my children were too young, why did my parents force me into science, the GFC, the city I lived in was too expensive, I had a mortgage, I couldn't afford to make a change. I just had to get through this period of my life. Over time, I became increasingly frustrated and fearful. Anxiety clouded my judgement and kept me anchored in my situation.

When we are in pain, we look for the fastest way to take our pain away. If the job is too painful, we assume another job is the solution. It seems completely logical. Get rid of the source of our unhappiness, then we will be happy, right?

The problem with this approach is it largely focuses on external factors. Our external situation is only half the equation. How you respond to it is the other. If we're not in control, we become a slave to external circumstances.

Getting away from toxic environments does give you space to think. Taking time out to rest and regroup is necessary for our wellbeing; however, unless we also take the time to reflect and learn, it's likely we will find ourselves in similar adverse situations again and again.

It's important you learn to reflect on and accept how you have contributed to your external environment; otherwise, the same stressful situations will emerge time and time again, even after you have landed a better job or started a passion business. Once the initial honeymoon period wears off, we often go back to the exact same place and problems with no change whatsoever.

To hope everything will change when the external environment changes gives your power away. As you change internally, you will be surprised to see how everything else starts to change as well. Meaningful change always starts with you.

Our current situation is the result of our long-term behavior, mindset and habits

Through my work, I have observed four primary habits that culminate in what I call "High Achievers Complex". As you read through these habits in the next section, you might relate to some of them or all of them. When I work with my clients, most can relate to them all.

These habits often give us the successes early on, but later lead to confusion and stagnation. Realising this was a huge discovery for me as for a long time, I didn't understand what I had done wrong to get to breaking point. I felt I had been a responsible, diligent person following all the rules. But as leadership expert Marshall Goldsmith says, "What got you here won't get you there."

These kinds of behaviours are our "superpowers" – that is until they stop working and derail our performance.

The four habits of high achievers

1. Care too much

We have pursued goals relentlessly often based on the expectations of others – Over time, this leads us to loss of *autonomy*

Our moment of awakening usually starts with the sense of "How did I end up here? Is this what I really want?" High achievers are often highly responsible people. They try to do the "right" things, but their decisions and actions can be based on the expectations of others or what society says is right. They might be good at achieving great things in life, but that doesn't mean they always head in the right direction or pursue a path that makes them happy.

Responsible people are often great leaders at home and in the workplace. Being responsible and considerate of others can bring us early successes. However, if we overly rely on this habit, our self-worth can become attached to what others think of us and, gradually, we lose touch with ourselves. Pleasing everybody ends up pleasing nobody. As we become overwhelmed by our responsibilities and the perfect image we believe we need to keep up with, we start to lose direction. Our performance drops and our stress level increases.

2. Be multi-talented

We have often achieved success without focusing on our strengths – Over time, this leads us to loss of *conviction*

Many intelligent people can learn new things with ease. Their ability to excel in many areas often enables them to climb the career ladder quickly, even in jobs they have no interest in. Corporations, like schools, value diversification and expect their workforce to be good at many things. However, if intelligent people strive to be good at everything without developing a deep understanding of what their real strengths are, they risk heading down the wrong path and under-utilising their capabilities.

Over time, they start to spend more time in the areas they are not naturally good at. Once a high performer, they struggle to keep up and gradually go from thriving to surviving. They might look like a shiny ball of confidence and success from the outside, they may have plenty of qualifications and skills and others may have told them they are highly capable. However, as they veer further away from their innate talents and strengths, their drive and performance start to decline as they see more of their faults, which creates self-doubt and impacts their confidence.

3. Do too much

We have worked hard to achieve our goals often feeling stressed at the same time – Over time, this leads us to loss of *wellness*

Workaholism is another habit that stops working in our favour. Working exceptionally hard often rewards us with success early in our career, but eventually wreaks havoc mentally and physically. We feel overwhelmed and exhausted by the demands and complexity of our work and life. Many of us are overworked yet find it difficult to slow down.

Carrying the motto "no pain, no gain", the high achievers are strong yet sometimes confuse stubbornness with resilience, pushing and struggling through life without pausing to adjust their tactics accordingly. They are the ones people look up to and rely on when the going gets tough. They might look after everybody else, but they often forget to look after themselves. Stress and unhealthy habits eventually impact their health and wellbeing. They want to have more calmness, balance and energy in their life but they don't know a better way of doing things.

4. Be single-minded

We have planned our life ahead diligently often in a very singular way – Over time, this leads us to loss of *passion*

Many high achievers achieve success early on because they can stay focused on their goals. While some of their peers scatter their efforts on various adventures, they know the fastest way to achieve success is to stay focused on the goals ahead. They lead a steady and secure life others envy.

However, they can be too single minded and often put their creative pursuits or passion projects on hold, concerned they might distract them from their safe and steady path. They are serious grown-ups! Without tapping into their passions and creativity, life feels dull, unexciting and repetitive. This will eventually make them feel resentful towards their daily work and life. Over time, their fire and joy dim. But a niggling voice inside asks them to re-connect with their life aspirations.

Reflection

- Which habit do you relate to the most?

You have not gone insane simply because you wake up one day feeling deeply unhappy and start to question your life, what has gone missing are some fundamental elements we need to feel fulfilled and alive: *autonomy, conviction, wellness and passion*. In the pursuit of ambitious goals, people tend to lose sight of these elements. It's difficult to be happy when these components are largely missing in your life.

When we overly rely on one set of behaviours, we lose the flexibility to adapt. Our needs and priorities change as we grow and mature. What worked for us in our youth won't always work as we enter our 30s, 40s and so on. If we don't learn to adapt, if we continue to engage in the same behaviours and mindset, we will remain where we are.

To make change, we need to break away from old beliefs and behaviours that no longer serve you and replace them with healthier, more effective strategies and habits.

We all have control over our lives

No matter how bad or hopeless our situation seems, we always have control over it. While imprisoned in the Auschwitz concentration camp during World War II, Viktor Frankl wrote his famous book, *Man's Search For Meaning*, in which he shared his observations and experiences of survival. Frankl saw people around him die every day; it seemed there was no hope. Yet he stressed the importance of focusing on one's purpose in life to survive.

Amid mass-scale genocide, starvation, torture and gas chambers, Frankl chose to ponder and write about the meaning of life. I am sure while writing his book he didn't think it was going to be a New York Times bestseller – he didn't even know if he would live another day. That was outside of his control. But one thing he did have control over was his thinking, his ability to observe and write every day, and his ability to find a worthwhile purpose. Nobody could give him hope except himself and he learned to improve his everyday situation by writing.

Frankl learned that the meaning of life is in every moment of living. He observed how some people were consumed by hopelessness and killed themselves before being killed by someone else, yet others were able to find meaning and small joys in the worst possible situations.

Like Frankl, when my father was working as a hard labourer in the remote farm, his passion for mathematics stayed strong. Instead of making his situation worse by feeling depressed and resentful, my dad decided to study maths during his spare time. He did this not because he wanted to be a mathematician one day – he had no idea when the

Cultural Revolution would end. But doing something he enjoyed made each day a little more enjoyable. It gave him hope and energy and exercised his mental agility so his mind stayed sharp. Ten years later, when he was eventually let go, he was one of the first to sit a university entrance exam at the mature age of 28.

Despite being robbed of 10 of his best years and being much older than his fellow university students, he became a well-known mathematician and the youngest professor in his university. His decision to study wasn't based on a desire to get ahead. This thinking would have caused him frustration and resentment. Rather, the point of his study was to create his own source of joy every day, which meant he had enough fuel in the tank to embrace opportunity when it did arrive.

The reality is, the longer you delay making positive changes to your current situation, the more defeated you will feel and the less willpower you will have to make the change. The idea we are powerless over our lives impacts our performance, decision-making capacity and wellbeing, so we feel worse about ourselves.

Raising the standard of our life starts with raising our standard of today. Despite how challenging your situation may be, it's important to ask yourself what you can do to improve today. This will take you from hopeless to hopeful.

The makings of living with more meaning and joy – Living Well Today

Happiness doesn't have to be the sacrifice we make to achieve success. We do not need to turn our life upside down to achieve a better, more meaningful and enjoyable life. It's about being aware of your blind spots and refining the habits that have brought you success but derailed your happiness. You can achieve success in a healthier way – this is the real success.

Living with more meaning and joy requires a re-balancing act. We need to start changing the way we live with four practices. I have named the framework as Living Well Today as I hope the four practices will act as a daily reminder of how effective you are living, so you have the *autonomy, conviction, wellness, and passion* you need each day. The focus is to learn to reshape how you work and live every day. This is a far gentler and more enjoyable way of improving your life.

When you become super clear about what motivates you and how you want to live your life, when you have unwavering trust in your decisions and capabilities, you will be able to create your own path and live a more inspired life with clarity and conviction.

I have created a four-step framework that will help you start making transformational changes in your life and work. In each following chapter, you will learn proven and research-based strategies that you can implement in real life.

These four practices will help you amplify the strengths you already have and break down the barriers that have held you back.

Practice 1: Care Less
Practice 2: More Strength
Practice 3: Do Less
Practice 4: More Passion

1. Care Less is about regaining control, identity and autonomy

We carry burdens every day. What do others think of me? How would I look if I failed? Will I let people down? These are enormous burdens to carry, preventing us from living the life we truly want to live. Learning to regain control and autonomy brings enormous freedom.

In this practice, you will learn how to:
- Let go of the pride armour
- Break away from expectations that no longer serve you
- Redesign your life priorities
- Be courageous to speak the truth and be your true self
- Eliminate non-essentials to make room for what truly matters

Care Less will allow you to break away from the anchors that have held you back in your life. It will create spaciousness in your mind so you can connect with what truly matters to you. You will find a new sense of clarity, control and peace.

2. More Strength is about building self-belief, self-acceptance and conviction

We are our biggest critic. If we don't know how to value and accept ourselves, if we don't focus on what's right and we don't know how to motivate ourselves on a day-to-day basis, no amount of external acknowledgement or rewards will make us feel happy and secure.

In this practice, you will learn how to:
- Make the most of your gifts
- Build self-belief and confidence like you never had before.
- Understand why you don't feel enough despite the fact you are highly capable
- Leverage your strengths to transform your career and life
- Be in tune with your unique strengths and Inner Genius

More strength will allow you to put an expiry date on the deep-seated, self-limiting beliefs that no longer serve you. You will be able to step out of the shadows and fully own and accept the brilliant version of you.

3. Do Less is about achieving wellbeing, daily restoration and optimal performance

To feel well, we must be well. If you learn how to maintain and optimise your level of energy and wellness every day, you will naturally feel happier and ready to embrace the next day. You will continuously enjoy life and make meaningful progress.

In this practice, you will learn how to:
- Master the art of "Do Less and Achieve More"
- Reshape your routines to achieve superior productivity
- Adopt the habits of peak performance
- Restore your energy and optimal state daily
- Be mindful of where you invest your energy and time

Do less will allow you to relinquish unhealthy working habits and be more in tune with your physical and mental wellbeing. This new way of working will reveal a new level of productivity, mental agility, and peak performance.

4. More Passion is about rediscovering your sense of fun, joy and creativity

We often put our passions and aspirations on hold unless we can turn them into a living. We then wonder why our joy disappears. We don't always have to choose between our profession and our passion – you can bring passion into your life and pursue your aspirations in many creative ways.

> In this practice, you will learn how to:
> - Leverage joy as a greater way to achieving results
> - Embrace passion projects to transform your work and life
> - Create joy on a daily basis
> - Combine passion with living
> - Contribute to the world around you and create meaningful experiences

More passion will allow you to tap into your inner creativity. You will let go of the perfectionism that prevents you from embracing new and exciting challenges. You will inject a new level of joy and energy into your life.

It's your life, so take control

A successful future is the sum of the conscious choices we make and the actions we take each day. The four practice areas act as a daily reminder of how effective you are living so you have the *autonomy, conviction, wellness, and passion* you need each day.

It allows daily opportunities to initiate, improve and invigorate. It creates a space for you to check in with yourself honestly – did I live well today? It helps you be mindful of the choices and actions you take daily. Instead of waiting for a New Year's resolution, you give yourself opportunities throughout the year to reset and renew yourself. The growth and satisfaction you will experience by taking this approach will be enormous.

All four principles in this book will help you change today's situation in an effective, easy-to-do manner, so you can see results quickly. Almost all of us have a vision for our life, but it's the actions we take and the healthy habits and mindset we build that turn it into reality. To transform the way you feel, you can simply start by changing how you live today.

....

Reflection

- What was one thing you thought was outside your control now you believe it is up to you to make the change?

....

How do you make the most of each practice area?

In each chapter, I will first share with you the content coupled with occasional reflection questions for you to work through the process. At the end of each chapter, there is a daily practice section reminding you to check in with yourself every day how you went in that particular practice area. Over time, and it won't take you long, you will start to notice the difference in you.

My recommendation is for you to read the rest of book first, then choose one practice area you find most relevant and practice that area for 30 days before you move onto the next practice. Habit building requires consistency in small doses: one change at a time, one habit at a time.

....

I have designed a free workbook to help you reflect as you go through each chapter. You can download it here
www.yudanshi.com/comealiveworkbook

PART III

FOUR PRACTICES

4
Care Less

When I let go of what I am,
I become what I might be.
LAO TZU

During my journey of change, I learned something profound: the more I accepted who I was, the less I cared about the things that didn't matter, the happier I became.

In an ironic way, I used to think I could only achieve success if I worked obsessively. In reality, as Viktor Frankl writes in his book *Man's Search for Meaning*: success will follow you precisely because you forget to think about it.

Essentially, Care Less is about being courageous and truthful: letting go the concern how others think of us and live a life more authentically. It is about being mindful where we invest our energy and time. This allows for spaciousness in our life and fill it with more of what matters.

Let go of our pride armour

As we begin this journey of change, one of the hardest things to deal with is how to reconcile our old identity with our new identity, especially when your new identity is still unclear and fragile. Despite how much we didn't enjoy the old identity, our pride, success and social acceptance were often attached to it.

These attachments often keep us in the rat race and prevent us from pursuing our new path wholeheartedly. We worry what others will think of us. At the heart of this is our need to look good, to look right. We want to send a message to the world that "we have it all together".

I was very attached to the identity that came with my job. The job was destroying my spirit yet at the same time I was hopelessly dependent on it. I could hide my insecurities under my business card. I felt lost without the armour of my title. "Who am I if I let this go? Am I now this aimless, depleted human being who has no clue what to do next?". My entire self-worth and identity were squarely attached to my job. I didn't know who I was or what my self-worth was without this external validation.

Leaving my job with nothing lined up presented me with a dilemma: how do I answer the question, "What do you do?". I had become used to introducing myself in my position. I didn't know how to describe myself anymore. I couldn't tell the truth that I was completely lost about my direction in life. It was difficult for me to say

I wasn't working and I was searching for the next step. More questions would follow and I couldn't answer them.

My ego compelled me to pretend I was executing a grand plan, even better than my last role, otherwise I would sound like a lunatic. As awful as it sounds, I still felt pride in what I was doing, despite the fact I was miserable and had no interest in my work.

On the one hand, I was curious and eager to explore opportunities; on the other, I was dealing with confusion and loss. By letting pride take over, I was diverted from the real task at hand – finding a new way of living. To protect my fragile ego, I wasted time and gave myself more to worry about in the process.

I spent a lot of energy worrying about what others thought of my actions instead of using the time to explore my options and make decisions about my life in a positive and creative way. I rarely asked for people's help, advice and input. I didn't want to admit I was lost and needed direction. Many people would have loved to help me.

In Carol Dweck's book, *Mindset,* she describes two different, opposing mindsets: a growth mindset and a fixed mindset. A growth mindset allows a person to see setbacks or failures as merely stepping stones towards growth and learning. The person with a growth mindset doesn't see themselves as stupid when they make a mistake. They believe they can always improve and progress. On the other hand, those with a fixed mindset don't believe change is possible. Everything is set in stone: "I did this once, therefore I am this forever." Making a mistake equals being stupid. Hence, they cannot afford to make any mistakes or be less than perfect. A person with a fixed mindset doesn't believe growth or progress is possible. This is usually the reason why people are so attached to being right and looking good.

One concept that strikes me the most is that the people with a growth mindset are not afraid to look bad or stupid. It's the people with a fixed mindset who always want to sound right, intelligent and look good.

I thought I had a growth mindset because I loved learning. But I realise now I couldn't face the prospect of needing help because my fixed mindset dictated that I should have all the answers and be in control at all times. When our focus is to look good and sound right, we effectively shut down our opportunities to learn more. When we constantly tell others we have got it all together, we close the door to any new suggestions and different ways of doing things. It limits our growth and potential.

Growth mindset helps pave the way to a new path

The desire to look good and be right limits our progress. The much faster way to move forward is to have a growth mindset and admit we don't have all the answers. It's OK to get help.

Once I realised this, I actively sought people I could learn from and who could help me brainstorm ways of moving forward. It only took a couple of meetings for me to come up with some options I could test straight away. One option was to do a three-day short course in coaching to see whether I truly enjoyed it and whether it was the right fit for me. Instead of agonising about the future and investing money into a premature business idea, three days was all I needed to test the water. I loved it and to this day, I am actively involved in the community that trained me to be an executive coach.

The other option was to talk to a career coach. I detested this idea at first because I felt like I should have been able to figure it out myself. However, my friend Sharon called me and almost demanded me to go. In her words, "How is it going to hurt you just by doing one session? You have been sitting on your hands for months." I went and immediately fell in love with my career coach (at a mental level, of course!). The process of self-discovery and her assessment lifted all my confusion. I was so enthusiastic about it that a week later, I was offered a contract with the organisation as senior career coach myself.

Although I eventually went back to my corporate executive role, the six-month experiment as a career coach and three-day coaching training opened a whole new world to me, which eventually led me to study my Master of Coaching Psychology. I gradually transitioned into senior corporate roles that aligned with my natural strengths, without having to start over.

I can almost guarantee that I wouldn't have made this progress if I hadn't sought the help I needed.

During the journey that followed, I learned to carry this growth mindset forward and never felt foolish to admit when I didn't have all the answers. I let my pride go and learned a new and accelerated way of growing and managing change. When I went back to my leadership roles, I was a much more effective leader. As I accepted help more readily from others, it significantly reduced my stress and working hours. People also felt less nervous around me as we could be more open about what we knew and what we didn't know. I was also more accepting of failure and incorporated more experimentation into my operating rhythm, as I realised my old perfectionist ways had stopped me and everybody else from being brave and more innovative.

This same approach also helped me set up my own business. I sought mentors before I started and factored in a failure rate. This allowed me to let go of my fear and I saw failure as part of the growth process. It gave me permission to experiment and stay creative.

When asked about his secret to success, Seth Godin, author of *Purple Cow*, said: "I think it's fair to say that I have failed more than most people. And I'm super proud of that. Part of the rules of this game is, the person who fails the most wins."

Reflection

- How does pride limit your growth?
- What do you need to do to stop looking good all the time?

We care so much how we show up that we could end up not showing up at all

One common barrier that has prevented people from trying new things in life is fear. But underneath that fear talk, if you look more closely, the concern is more about their pride: "What would people think of me? What if I fail, how would that make me look?" It's this need to look good and care too much about what others think stops us from experimenting and growing.

Fear loves the status quo. If you stay in your comfort zone, fear will not haunt you. However, fear kills aspiration, joy and stops us from experiencing life fully.

Harper Lee wrote *To Kill a Mockingbird* while she was still a young, unpublished author. It immediately became a critically-acclaimed success, winning the 1961 Pulitzer Prize. Generations later, it is still a classic of modern American literature, loved by millions of people around the world. Lee didn't publish another book until 2015, *Go Set a Watchman*. Why did such a talented, gifted novelist wait so long to write another book? Her answer was fear.

"I never expected any sort of success with Mockingbird," Lee said during an interview with radio host Roy Newquist in 1964. "I was hoping for a quick and merciful death at the hands of the reviewers, but at the same time, I sort of hoped someone would like it enough to give me encouragement. Public encouragement. I hoped for a little, as I said, but I got rather a whole lot, and in some ways, this was just about as frightening as the quick, merciful death I'd expected."

Lee feared she would never be able to replicate her success or produce such a transcendental masterpiece again. What a tragedy for us all. She could not share her gift with the world for so long because of her own fear.

Let me tell you another story. Elizabeth Gilbert wrote the book *Eat, Pray, Love*. Like Harper Lee's *Mockingbird*, it also became an overnight bestseller. And, like Lee, Gilbert faced the same fear as a newly celebrated author. In her 2014 Ted Talk, she said people would regularly ask her: "How could you ever replicate the success you achieved with Eat, Pray, Love?"

She decided that writing brought her joy, so she was going to write regardless of the outcome. It was true none of her following books gave her as much success as the first book, but she kept writing because it was her passion and inner genius. *She was doing it for herself, not anyone else.*

Several books later, Gilbert wrote *Big Magic*, published in 2015. In this book, she examines the creative process and the mystery of inspiration, which she calls "creative genius". Like *Eat, Pray, Love*, this book was an instant success. Oprah Winfrey named Gilbert as one of the top 10 most inspirational people. What would have happened if she had let fear stop her from sharing her joy and gifts?

Do you choose to live your life in fear or do you choose to live your life in spite of fear? Is it more important to share your gifts, which bring you joy, or is it more important to hide your gifts for fear that others will not appreciate them? There is always a choice in life.

Living in fear is not living at all

As J.K. Rowling, author of the *Harry Potter* series, famously said in her 2008 commencement speech at Harvard University, *"It is impossible to live without failing at something, unless you live so cautiously that you might as well not have lived at all, in which case you have failed by default."*

Self-determination is the essence of freedom

Our struggle and search for our identity and direction often come from trying to break away from social norms while also trying to stay connected to society. We try to balance what we want with what is expected of us.

To progress and survive, we do need external successes. The

economic reality is that we need to find a job or start a business to generate an income. We can't escape the reality of living and working within these confines. But a person doesn't need to conform to every social norm. Having independent ideas, needs, preferences, talents and goals is part of what it means to be an individual and to make a unique contribution to the fabric of society.

To grow as a person, you embark on a process of developing your own ideas and priorities while separating yourself from some of the external ideas and pressures that don't serve your needs.

Learning to enjoy this freedom means rejecting some social pressures. Warren Buffett is one of the richest people in the world, yet he lived in his standard family homes for decades, because he is not attached to the traditional image of success. When we choose to be less attached to social norms, it gives us the freedom to put more energy into the things that do matter to us.

Challenging social norms and external pressures is liberating but it takes courage. In my case, defying the social norm of having a prestigious job meant defying my parents, who had encouraged me in that direction for so long in the hope I would have a better life. Can you give yourself permission to defy the people who have instilled these beliefs in you? In other words, do you believe you have what it takes to live a successful and fulfilling life by following your own path?

As we break free from social pressures, we regain control and autonomy. The success you create for yourself is vastly more satisfying and more valuable than the success others want for you. Self-determination is the essence of freedom.

Reset your priority

How would you live differently if you only had one year to live? My defining moment taught me how precious time is. Almost everything can be made back except time. Once it's gone, it's gone.

I once asked a friend who was at a crossroads in her career what she would do if she only had one year to live. She knew the answer almost immediately. So, one question I ask myself often is, "What decisions would I make if I only had one year to live?". I have found asking this question helps reset my priorities.

If your goal is to feel more fulfilled and happier, create a new set of criteria and let this guide you. Don't let your ego decide because ego thrives on the opposite set of criteria. Pursuing a career path for the wrong priority will likely result in you resenting the responsibility, long hours or other parts of the deal you didn't want. You may lose interest and underperform in the role. Your success will likely be a short-lived one and you will be miserable. Being miserable is not a success, no matter how much you earn or how high up you are. If you hate your job, that is not a success story.

If you know what your true priority is, you can steer your career and life choices in this direction. When I went back to my marketing executive role for the second time, for a different company but in the same tech industry, I made sure my priority was my wellbeing, my family and that I could contribute more meaningfully to my team, organization and the industry. This reset how I worked and spent my time and it re-energised me completely.

What are your priorities in life?

Stop playing the ineffective games

Small or large, we all have our own games to survive and to impress: arriving at work before the boss and leaving after the boss; working through our lunch breaks to appear more dedicated or more overloaded than we are; replying to emails late at night; telling everyone how busy we are.

The problem is, most of these false-impression tactics don't serve us at all. None of these fake behaviours impresses anyone. Your true value is in what and how you contribute, not how busy and important you appear to be.

After my illness, I stopped trying to convince people I was busy and important. I began to focus on being more effective and efficient. I was able to improve my productivity dramatically simply by changing this one behaviour. It was a revelation to me and I immediately saw how much more I got done. More importantly, my results were better because my mind was no longer occupied by fake tactics.

The most powerful moment came when I realised I had significantly reduced my working hours but I had no intention of staying in the office longer or doing a second shift after putting my kids to bed just to show my managers how dedicated I was. If I finished all the work I had set out to do for the day, I went home and enjoyed myself with my family or went for a late-afternoon walk. These things help us stay motivated much longer and restore our energy immediately, something we will explore in Chapter 6.

I stopped working long hours and encouraged others to do the same. No one lost their jobs for "*appearing*" less dedicated and over-worked. However, you can lose your job if you perform poorly. We live in a results-driven economy. At the end of the day, an organisational result depends on the result the workforce delivers, not the pretending tactics they play. These games simply encourage a stressed and anxious workforce.

Reflection

- Do you waste time on meaningless tactics?

Less attachment produces better outcome

When you stop playing games to get ahead, you will get ahead faster. It is counter-intuitive but true. Have you ever had the experience of wanting something so badly, but it only arrives once you let go of the expectation? How often does something land on your lap when you least expect it, then once you become obsessed with it, it stalls or disappears altogether?

Desperation creates anxiety and stress. The less attached we are to the outcome, the more relaxed and positive we feel and the better we can perform. When there is easiness around an outcome, other people can feel it, too, and things come together more easily.

One of my clients, Wendy, said she felt free once she started to let go of her attachment to her pride. She became braver in approaching people who were more senior than her both inside and outside organisations; she started to ask "dumb" questions openly at meetings without worrying how she might have looked; she proposed much more innovative ideas because her joy of doing something amazing had taken over her fear of failure. She gained new knowledge and experiences by leaps and bounds through these actions. She said she was also surprised how simple things like that earned so much respect from others.

As she let her guard down, people felt more comfortable around her and involved her in more opportunities. In return, bigger and better opportunities came her way. She won competitions, got invited to be a guest speaker in industry events and was given a significant seeding fund by her organisation to start a dream project. Only six months earlier, nobody had heard of her in the industry. She also turned her personal life around. She now rarely does late-night work and enjoys a happier family life.

Essentially, she doubled her outcome by working half the time.

Our performance always improves as we become less attached to the outcome. Focusing more on what truly matters elicits the best from us. Constantly obsessing with what others think and worrying about things that don't produce results saps our energy, leaving little room for us to do our best work.

Eliminate the non-essentials

As I was wheeled into the operating room, most of the things I had cared so much about the day before felt childish and meaningless. At the time, it caused a deep sense of regret and remorse.

When you do an audit of your life, I bet you will find you waste so much time on meaningless stuff and worry about things that don't matter. If your time can be better spent, you will be a lot happier.

The good news is, we can make a choice about how we spend our time and what we focus on.

The non-essentials tend to be unnecessary worries and distractions, such as:

- What other people think about you
- Having everything your peers have – luxury cars, holiday homes, designer handbags
- Pleasing others at the cost of your happiness
- Making time for people who are draining and toxic
- Saying yes to unimportant things because you are afraid of what will happen if you say no
- Spending too much time on devices and mindless Internet browsing

Saying yes to the essential things only is empowering. It's one simple step towards regaining control and defining your self-worth. Narrowing the list of the essentials in your life will allow you to choose where to focus your time and energy. When we eliminate everything that doesn't matter to us, we make room for the things that do.

The essentials could be things that bring you joy and meaning, such as:

- Creating value for others
- Making time for the people you love and care about
- Spending time each day doing things that bring you joy
- Making the most of your time and maximising your contribution

- Saying yes to new opportunities
- Investing time in building quality relationships

Take notice of how you spend your time over the course of a week and you will see how much time you could save on the non-essentials. Then, focus on how you spend your time over the course of a day. Pay attention to how you can make a difference to your enjoyment and experience of today by simply saying no to the non-essentials.

Reflection

- What non-essentials do you need to stop focusing on?
- What essentials deserve more of your time?

Communicate your intent clearly

It's quite common to see people whose actions contradict their intentions. For instance, they might say yes to a promotion they no longer want. Their behaviour not only confuses themselves, it also confuses others. It's like putting one foot on the break and the other on the accelerator – you will go nowhere. People can only help you and give you what you want if you act accordingly.

Of course, I played this game as well. Several times, I told the company that I would relocate for the right job. Mobility is something global companies value in their key talent. While I loved experiencing different cultures, I was happiest when I was at home in Sydney.

Moving to another country didn't excite me. But for years, I would tick yes to total mobility. I thought I had to say yes in order to be valued.

When I finally told the truth, it wasn't a career-limiting move. I was still given opportunities and I was able to look after multiple countries in a variety of roles from my Sydney base. It was a revelation to me that it was possible to be honest about my priorities without negative repercussions. In fact, once the pressure disappeared, it allowed me to have more open discussions and the freedom to embrace opportunities I genuinely wanted to pursue in and outside of work.

Of course, I had already decided my priority was to have freedom in my work and to lead passion-based projects. Yours might be different. If your priority is to gain experiences in different countries at a more hands-on level, then being mobile is something you will likely need to be. Our priorities guide our decisions.

Clear and honest communication shows we have confidence in ourselves. We shift the focus from cookie-cutter behaviour to more lasting results and qualities. I genuinely believe that people respect honesty. Being clear about your priorities and focus is refreshing and respected. It distinguishes you from the norm. Honesty saves time, stops us from playing games and is an assuring quality that encourages people around you to behave the same way.

Show up honestly

One year after my journey began, my friend Julia was a guest speaker at an event I hosted. She shared her heartache around her disabled daughter and her marriage breakdown. I was staggered to see how open she was, how she trusted a room full of strangers and revealed her vulnerability completely.

I always thought showing my vulnerability was a form of weakness: it meant I was not strong enough.

As a child, despite the many heartaches I experienced, I rarely cried. While my struggles showed me how harsh life could be, they also strengthened me. I was always hopeful. I saw the silver lining in every difficult situation. I viewed setbacks as opportunities for character building.

The downside of this was that I didn't allow myself to show any vulnerability. I found it difficult to be open. I believed I needed to get over my emotions quickly. I would cut my sadness short, bouncing back before anyone could feel sorry for me.

Looking at Julia, I didn't feel any weakness from her. To the contrary, I felt a real sense of strength, openness and courage from her.

I realised that for so long, I had been trying to keep up with this perfect image I had set for myself. I realised what I was really afraid of was showing my inadequacy.

When I was nine years old, after seeing me stare longingly through restaurant windows one too many times, Mum decided to take me to a restaurant for a meal. However, just before we entered the restaurant, I told Mum I was no longer hungry. I knew we couldn't afford the meal. I didn't want Mum to feel bad. I didn't want us to lose face. I never stood in front of a restaurant again until I was able to afford it myself many years later.

Without ever being explicitly told, I understood from a very young age not to show our lack of wealth in any way publicly.

Feeling inadequate isn't only associated with financial

limitations. Having worked with so many people, I have learned that almost all of us, no matter how underprivileged or privileged our upbringing might have been, we all feel inadequate in one way or another. Often, our drive to achieve isn't about being "great"; often, it is to cover our feelings of inadequacy, whether they are financial, emotional, mental or physical. We want to achieve more so we feel more adequate, worthy and complete.

This desire to do more, be more, might seem to be a healthy dose of a drive to push ourselves to achieve greater things. However, if this drive comes from a place of inadequacy, it will eventually become a source of deep unhappiness.

At the heart of this is self-acceptance: permission to be happy without having all the achievements, qualifications, titles, money and status.

- Permission to experience moments of joy, even though we might not have ticked off every goal on life's checklist.
- Permission to celebrate even if we have failed splendidly. The courage to fail and our learnings as a result deserve celebration.
- Permission to indulge our passions, even if they don't give us an immediate financial return.
- Permission to experiment and fail without viewing failure as a statement about our real capabilities.
- Permission to take time out to look after ourselves without feeling guilty.
- Permission to say we are good enough.
- Permission to say we are worthy, even if we don't have as

many accolades as our peers.
- Permission to say we are capable, even if we haven't ticked every metric of success.

Flip your focus

Instead of wanting more and trying to achieve more to show the world you are good enough, imagine being proud of who you are no matter what, no matter how you might look based on external criteria.

You can be at ease with yourself. You can accept yourself fully.

If we could wake up every day knowing deep in our heart that all we have been given, all that is uniquely ours, are precious gifts, we would not take them for granted.

We would use our gifts for a greater purpose, not just to participate in a perpetual game of chase. We would treat our time much more wisely. Instead of spending time playing catch ups, we would be able to direct our energy and time to good causes.

The most fulfilled people have a purpose that is larger than themselves and value their contribution to others over fulfilling their own needs.

However, purpose doesn't always have to start from changing the world. It's an immense pressure to start with something this gigantic. I always feel changing the world can start from changing yourself, by giving yourself some meaning will naturally create changes around you.

When we care less about how we show up externally and care more about how we honestly feel, we can let go of our mask and become freer in our endeavours.

Reflection

- What decisions would you make if you only had one year to live?
- What change would you like to make in order to live more authentically?

Daily Practice

To strengthen the Care Less practice, you can simply ask yourself this one question:
- What was one thing I cared less about today?

At end of each day, you can also reflect quietly how you went today:
- How many things did I do today to look good?
- How many things did I do today really mattered to me?
- How many things did I do today without the concern of having to look good?

5
More Strength

Everybody is a genius. But if you judge a fish by it's ability to climb a tree, it will live its whole life believing that it is stupid.
ALBERT EINSTEIN

In the ground breaking research conducted by Jay Niblick, author of *What's Your Genius*, a common pattern was found amongst the most successful people. These people tend to invest most of their time using their natural strengths and find creative ways to make their weaknesses redundant. What sets them apart is their self-awareness and ability to make the most of what they already have.

Renowned leadership coach Marshall Goldsmith recounted in his interview with Niblick that from early in his career, he recognised he was good at only a few things. He decided he needed to focus on them fully to become masterful in them.

Yet many of us do the opposite. We spend more time fixing our weaknesses than developing our strengths.

We preoccupy ourselves with what we lack, what's "wrong" with us. I believe we could create a much more satisfying life by paying more attention to what's "right", what we already have.

Essentially, More Strength is about making the most of the natural and unique gifts we have today. We all have our inner genius, waiting to be discovered and utilised fully. More strength will allow you to put an expiry date on the deep-seated, self-limiting beliefs that no longer serve you and help you accept yourself wholeheartedly.

Career dissatisfaction doesn't happen overnight – it builds over time

The main cause of this is the feeling that one's talent is not being fully utilised. A recent survey from Insync shows that just one in nine people at corporations today strongly agree that their skills and talent are being used to their full potential. That's a staggering figure. We are talking about a lot of wasted talent and potential.

Research from Centre for Applied Positive Psychology shows that only 70% of the population can say what they are really good at in any meaningful way. If we don't know what our talents are, we could choose the wrong career, we might work in jobs that make us feel less competent, and we might not be able to make a meaningful contribution the way we wanted.

For me, the warning signs had been there for years. There was a huge misalignment between my natural talents and what was required of me in the jobs I took. Over the years, my marketing job had changed from a strategic, creative role to a more analytical one due to the change of market condition and the jobs I had chosen. I was required to spend time in many areas I was good at but simply didn't enjoy. Positive psychologist Dr Alex Linley calls these skillsets "learned behaviours" – skills that we have learned to be good at but will drain us if used too often.

I was good with numbers, but it was not something that I enjoyed doing all the time. Taking creativity and big picture thinking out of my day-to-day work and replacing it with numbers and spreadsheets was suffocating. To keep up and maintain the peace, I forced myself to suck it up and just do it. Despite my best efforts to stay positive, I felt drained constantly. I felt like a fish out of water.

I was always good with setting up new businesses, creating strategies and developing teams, except the operational side of my jobs sapped the energy out of me. Many of us spend a large amount of time performing learned behaviours, wondering why we are not happy. If learned behaviour becomes a major part of your key performance areas, linked to salary, bonuses and future promotions, you can feel trapped.

The higher I went, the more time I spent in my learned behavior zone. I didn't realise this at the time and believed I was incompetent. I didn't know how to get out of the cycle. Those learned skills led to higher promotions with higher salaries. Those were the carrots that kept me going.

Reflection

- What part of the job have you learned to be good at but drains you?

Strength approach comes to rescue

To climb back from rock bottom after my illness in 2008, I knew I had to do something completely different.

But I had a dilemma, I realised I knew nothing about myself. I had no idea what my real talent was. I was able to list many things I was good at but had no interest in. Then there were things I was interested in but didn't have the skills or experience.

I spoke to dozens of recruiters, and they all told me they could find me an identical job in a heartbeat but don't consider a different area. I believed that I had many transferrable skills, but they said most companies would prefer to hire people who wanted to stay in the same way. In another word, besides marketing jobs, I was practically unemployable.

But by then, I was determined to find an answer without turning my life upside down. I read many books and did a lot of research. I received insights but nothing resonated with me at a deep and practical level until 18 months after my operation, I finally came across an approach that ultimately changed my life, my career, everything.

The Realise2 Strengths approach created by Dr Alex Linley, a renowned positive psychologist, is based on the notion that we can only *sustain* our wellbeing and performance if we live in accordance with our authentic strengths.

Strengths are the things we are good at and come to us naturally. When we use them, we are in our element, and we feel at home. Strengths are our unique gifts. We feel naturally competent and confident when we use them. The number speaks for itself. A global study from the Corporate Leadership Council shows that employee performance increases by a staggering 60% if their leader focuses on their strengths instead of their weaknesses.

Linley's discovery is profound: not everything we are good at is necessarily our strength. Suddenly, everything made sense to me. How I approached my work was wrong. I had spent most of my career doing things that were not my natural strengths. I had learned to be good at my job only through working hard. I felt unhappy because every day, I turned up to work trying to be somebody I was not. I was good at what I did but it didn't come to me naturally. This was why I felt so unauthentic.

Natural power of strengths

A major concern I had at the time was that I believed I would have to spend another 15 – 20 years to get to a reasonable level in a different field. I couldn't imagine spending 20 years starting from scratch. What I didn't know was we could learn things exceptionally fast if they were our strengths. On the other hand, we will likely stagnate if we remain stuck in our non-strengths areas as eventually, our performance will decline.

Based on Linley, strength is a pre-existing capacity that already exists within us. We are either born with strengths or have developed them during our early years. They come to us easily and naturally. When we work with our strengths, we learn things faster and more effortlessly. They don't seem extraordinary to us, so we find them difficult to identify. For example, if you are naturally good with people, if you are creative or just know how to get things organised, you can do these things exceptionally well without any training. Others without these natural abilities would have to learn to be good at them.

I learned this lesson once I began coaching. I spent 20 years in studying and marketing computers, I only achieved average competency, and I felt quite incompetent in these areas most days. I struggled in all my computer science subjects during my undergraduate degree. Once I started learning psychology, I thrived. Learning was easy for me, and I completed my Master of Coaching Psychology within 2 years while working full time and was accepted into a doctoral program upon graduation. In fact, I did Excel training five times during my career and I still can barely do Macro. Yet I didn't have to learn how to coach, facilitate or be strategic. These skills come to me naturally.

When I attended my first coach certification course, my learning partner asked whether I had been doing this for a long time, but that was the first time I attended a formal training. I felt confident, happy, and energised after attending my coaching course, yet I felt dumb, drained, and disheartened just a few months earlier after attending a financial modelling course.

Can you relate to this? Can you find your own examples? What is something you always did with ease? What is something you have tried for a long time but your brain just doesn't get it no matter how hard you try?

When we don't work from our natural strengths, every task feels like a lot of effort, we max out quickly. No matter how hard we try, how smart we are or how determined we might be, we will hit the ceiling. To keep our performance up, we work even harder, only feel more exhausted, barely surviving. We lose our confidence and feel burned out.

As researcher Tom Rath notes in his book *Strength Finder*, the reality is that a person who has always struggled with numbers is unlikely to be a great accountant or statistician. While it is possible to improve your weakness, it is unlikely you will master it at the same level and speed compared to your strengths. This is what Niblick's research has discovered and why so many elite performers only work hard on their strengths.

Accepting our strengths is a courageous act

Accepting our strengths can work against some of the principles we have learned in life such as being humble; always looking for ways to fixing our weaknesses. Humans are critical of themselves in order to evolve and advance. We constantly look for something to improve to make our lives better. The problem with focusing on what we are not is that everything we are gets overlooked. No matter how great we are, how unique, how amazing, how gifted, how many abilities we have, we simply don't see these things and don't value them.

We sometimes find difficulty in recognising our strengths because we don't value things that come easily, we believe things are only worthwhile if we work hard for them. Teaching has always been easy for me, and it took me a long time to realise it was a gift. I used to think, "Doesn't everyone else do that, too? This is so easy." Whatever is easiest for you, in fact, is your greatest asset. If it comes to you easily without trying, can you imagine what it would be like if you focus on strengthening it?

Not accepting and focusing on our strengths is a missed opportunity for many of us. It not only leads to work dissatisfaction, poor choice of career, reduced productivity, but also the loss of self-belief. Have you ever felt dumb when you read one book yet felt competent reading another?

Would you prefer to spend time in mastering something or barely grasping? What a loss it would be if we have these strengths and gifts, yet we are not utilising them fully. In contrary, we spend our time and effort working in our weakest areas, things that would take us a much longer time to comprehend, excel and master. There is a little joy in it. Working hard can create result, but it produces even greater result when we direct our effort to our strengths.

Reflection

- What things come to you easily?
- What things do you enjoy doing?
- What activities do you find energising?

How do intelligent people lose confidence

Not using our strengths is one of the main reasons why intelligent people lose confidence. When I first started this journey, I realised I knew very little of myself. In fact, my perception of myself was negative and unhealthy. Despite my external achievements, I never felt satisfied with my talents. I didn't feel I was good enough. I am not alone; many people often focus on what's wrong instead of what's right about them. Often, we start this at a very young age without us even realising the consequence of it.

One of the deepest fear I had when I began my journey was I believed what I achieved could never be replicated. I felt I was lucky enough to be in my position and it was not possible to carve out a path based on my natural talents. This mindset came from a long standing perception of myself: I was not clever enough.

As a small child, I found learning easy. We didn't have a TV or any toys, so books were all I had. I was delighted when my mother decided to send me to school two years early, even though I was too short to sit on the chairs. I loved having the opportunity to read more books and school was easy for me. I loved everything about it.

My joy and love of learning ended abruptly when I moved to a new school in Grade 4. I was seven years old. The new school had a harsh maths teacher who would beat us with a bamboo stick. The beatings were indiscriminate, so you never knew when she would strike. Sometimes, she hit me so hard my hands would bleed.

I was terrified. Learning was no longer about the joy of reading and solving problems, it was about not making mistakes. I never raised my hand to ask a question, give an answer or show any interest. Even with my best attempts, I was beaten regularly.

Other teachers were brutal, too. In PE class, I was too small to keep up with my classmates. I loved running and always tried my hardest. One day, the PE teacher kicked me hard, completely out of the blue. The force was so strong, I fell to the ground bleeding.

The brutality of school made me very upset and confused. I was no longer the kid who loved every minute of school. I dreaded it. I was simply too little to fight back and I was terrified of the beatings. I was a good student, always polite and well-behaved. I knew it was not my fault but even so, I stayed quiet and tried to be invisible. School became a place I learned to survive.

On the first day of the summer holiday, Mum gave me six textbooks for Grade 5 and 6 Maths, Chinese and English. She told me if I could show her how clever I was and taught myself all six books, she would send me to high school. She told me there would be no play until I finish my designated study time each day. I was crushed to miss my holiday but I saw this as my way of escaping. I studied every day.

I was eight years old when I started high school. I was relieved my high-school teachers didn't beat me. I enjoyed every subject until I started learning physics and my whole world tumbled down. Physics confounded me. I found it difficult to comprehend any of the concepts. I felt like the dumbest kid. I tried hard to understand but my mind went blank whenever I looked at the textbooks.

When I demonstrated that I was able to keep up with the rigorous high-school schedule, I was viewed as a gifted child. I made my mum proud, as not many people agreed with my mum's approach. Remember, this was in the early 1980s, a time when many Chinese families favoured boys over girls in remote towns like ours. Nobody we knew placed so much emphasis on the education of their daughter. My high school was one of the best in the country and being selected to attend was like winning the lottery. The school produced many brilliant minds. Upon entering the school, we were told we were the future of this country and must succeed. We were all fiercely proud of our school and wanted to do our school, teachers and parents proud.

But when I started to struggle in physics, people said perhaps I shouldn't be there. Although I excelled in every other subject, I worried the school would kick me out and tell me I didn't deserve my place. My confidence flatlined. By the end of the year, not only did I fail physics, my other marks started to decline, as well. I went home with my results, filled with shame. My mother told me only really smart people could do well in physics. I have never forgotten her words that day. I was crushed. I had invested so much energy in improving my weakest subject, I didn't spend time on my stronger subjects. And after all my hard work, I had still failed. My mother was right.

Nobody stepped in and said, "Hey, you can't be good at everything. Don't worry!" I was told to try harder, so I did. The more I tried, the more frustrated I became. I had started my education as a fresh-faced four-year-old, utterly enraptured with learning. I was now anxious, terrified of failure and convinced of my innate stupidity and incompetence, all because of one subject.

Years later, whenever I was in situations that reminded me of that experience, I would freeze. My brain would automatically tell me I couldn't figure this out, it's too hard. At work, whenever people talked about complex science, I could feel myself get smaller. One minute, I was confident and articulate, the next minute, I had somehow shrunk and lost my voice.

What I didn't understand, nor did my mother or my teachers were that physics was not my natural strength, no matter how hard I tried, the improvement I would make on that subject was just not great. By giving me pressure to focus on my weakest subject derailed my confidence and entire school performance. Had I been encouraged to spend time developing my good subjects, not only I would have got a much better overall mark, but also it would have given me the confidence to manage physics more effectively.

Can you relate to this in some ways?

A universal habit

My story might have entailed some brutality but is not unique. In every culture Gallup has studied, most parents think a student's *lowest grades deserve the most time and attention.* Parents and teachers reward excellence with apathy rather than encouraging children to invest more time in the areas where they have the most potential for greatness.

Let's say little Jamie's natural strength is English and his weakness is maths. He comes home with an English score of 90 and a math score of 60. Most parents might give Jamie some praise for his good efforts in English but naturally start to shift focus to discuss ways for Jamie to improve his maths. Little Jamie learns the things he is naturally good at deserve little focus, appreciation and time. He also learns he is expected to be good at every subject, so instead of putting more effort in things he is naturally good at, Jamie now scatters his effort in everything.

When we go to work, we continue this pattern. We have been

told that to succeed, we need to be strategic, organized, creative, great at presentations and public speaking, have emotional intelligence and empathy. Honestly, are we all born superheroes? I don't know many creative people who can be organized at the same time. Given this common practice and attitude, is there any wonder why after 10, 20 or 30 years of working, we can hardly remember what our natural strengths are?

Once the talented Jamie now strives to be like everyone else, avergage at everything. We start to lose our own uniqueness, our independent edge.

Jack of all trades

We can't be good at everything. By trying to be, we become average at everything.

One common dilemma I have discovered while working with my clients is that despite all the qualifications and recognition they have, most people find it difficult to articulate what their unique talents are. One recurring comment I hear from people is, "I feel like I am a jack of all trades but master of none."

It's hard to understand your uniqueness after spending so many years following a success template that requires you to be like everyone else. This is why people often struggle to define their self-worth after years of working in large corporations. A lot of people would go as far to say they don't have any talents, despite the fact they have held their jobs steadily and successfully for decades and are often regarded highly by their peers and teams. When we all end up looking like each other on the paper, it is difficult to gain clarity and position yourself in your career or business.

We are not robots. Each of us has a unique combination of skills, talents and experiences. Understanding who we are and how to make the best use of our gifts is essential to our identity, happiness and self-worth. We might not be good at everything, but we can be exceptionally great in a few things. We can get things accomplished and achieve amazing results in our own unique and authentic ways.

Rewrite your past

We often let one negative experience influence how we perceive ourselves. In his book, *Authentic Happiness*, positive psychologist Dr Martin Seligman looks at what causes people to be either pessimistic or optimistic. He explains that the difference comes down to how we look at each event. When a single negative event occurs, if we perceive it as permanent and universal, we have over-exaggerated this event, which leads us to a helpless state. What we should have done was look at the event as temporary and specific.

We all have unpleasant memories. I know many strong and confident men and women who still get emotional when they recall an event that impacted them years ago. Most are not traumatic, most are experiences almost all of us had as we grew up. Yet to these men and women, these experiences are personal. It could be that they forgot what they were going to say the first time they had to make a public speech in primary school. Perhaps they got teased for being too smart. Often, they are surprised by how emotional they still feel about the memory and would say that overall, they had a normal childhood.

Rebecca broke down at my workshop when I was giving this

example. She said she only now realised why she always chose to be invisible. She was a very bright child but she got teased once by her classmates for being too bright. Trying to fit in, she started telling herself to stop saying smart things. She ended up doing that for 30 more years. She used to get frustrated that she had to work for people who are less talented than her, but not until the workshop, did she realise that actually it was herself keep telling her to stay low, not just at work, every area in her life.

It's not about if you had a good or bad childhood, it's how you had interpreted the events. I can now see how clearly this past event at school and all the events that followed were affecting me. Instead of treating each event as a situational event, I had taken them to heart. Since failing in physics, I had often focused on what was "wrong" with me. It had become a way of life.

Even on this journey looking for an alternative career, every single idea was based on what I didn't have. I never paused to think, "Well, what could I do with everything I've already got?" The only things I considered were things I didn't have the skillsets for, so therefore I would need to retrain and start at the bottom again.

I had carried this feeling of being dumb for almost 25 years. No matter how much recognition I got, how many promotions, degrees, awards I received, deep down, I never felt I was good enough. When things were going well, I would be OK. When things didn't go well, I would immediately feel like an imposter.

I had embarked on a journey to find a career I felt passionate about and wanted to do. My biggest discovery was, it was not finding out what I *wanted to do*. It was finding the courage and self-belief to know I *can do* it. What was standing in my way was myself.

Feeling competent is key to satisfying work, as Daniel Pink explains. His research on human motivation and drive shows that having a sense of competency is one of the most critical factors in adult working life. Not feeling competent can hold people back from pursuing their goals and aspirations. Even when we have all the skill-sets, qualifications and experiences required, our often harmful perception of ourselves prevents us from making change. It's not because we are not clever enough or good enough, it's because we *don't feel* we are clever enough or good enough.

As Dr Anthony Grant says in his book, *Coach Yourself,* our minds can develop many automatic beliefs, however, some of these feelings are real but not *reality*. Negative self-talk can be built up over years. Every time we have failed at something, been criticised or felt stupid, we have added to our negative self-talk.

Many of us haven't grown up with cheerleaders, even with the best intent, our parents and teachers might not have given us the support and encouragement we needed. My client Carl said to me one day that he had finally realised he needed to be that cheerleader for himself.

Change how we perceive ourselves

How we perceive our abilities plays a critical role in whether we will succeed or fail in our endeavours. I realised I needed to do much more than finding the perfect job. I also needed to know myself more deeply and resolve my perceptions of myself. Otherwise, my negative self-beliefs would always hold me back.

We can change how we perceive ourselves. It's true, we can't change what happened in the past. I cannot deny the abuse, bullying and failure I experienced. I also can't pretend these experiences weren't painful and traumatic. We all have scars. But what we can change is the way these past experiences influence the way we think of ourselves and act in the present. By changing our perception of negative events, we can create more positive actions and thoughts.

Negative experiences don't define us forever. Can you think of an alternative viewpoint or evidence to prove your assumptions are not true? If I think of all the positive experiences I had at school instead of the negative, the evidence is irrefutable.

My job might not have been 100% aligned with my natural strengths. However, the way I viewed myself and my talents was completely within my control. I realised how insane it was to spend years in areas I would never flourish in, where I would perform far below my real capability. I devalued my gifts and overvalued my weakest abilities, just like I did in high school. My natural strength were valuable. I was not an expert in technology but I was a competent leader with many unique capabilities which made me a good leader over the years.

My biggest realisation was that instead of giving up my career, I needed to give up my weakness and let my natural strengths shine.

....

Reflection

- What one weakness you can start to let it go?
- What one strength you can start to let it shine?

....

Let your strengths shine

In my first CMO role, I focused on the mountain of work assigned to me. In my second CMO role which was essentially the same as my old one, I became incredibly aware of my strengths and learned behaviour.

I crafted the role and designed my days to maximise my strengths. I also encouraged my teams to help each other based on their strengths. Dr Alex Linley calls this complementary partnering. Nobody goes to work just to feel dreadful, but it's a leader's role to ensure everybody gets to maximise their talents and enjoy his or her work.

At work, I found complementary colleagues who loved doing things that were not my natural strengths. In turn, I would help them with my strengths to get their jobs done. I learned that what was boring to me could be interesting to others and what was stressful for me was easy for others. All I needed to do was ask.

Do you know the strengths of others?

I also actively sought out activities aligned with my strengths. I joined in a mentoring program to offer my time in mentoring talents in the industry. At work, I volunteered to coach others and I put my hand up for a talent development project.

In the past, I would never have done that as I would have worried about other people thinking I was "wasting time" outside my role. But I wasn't worried at all. I wanted to do it because I knew I would enjoy it and add value to others. I learned that the more enjoyment I brought to work, the more productive I became. I made a greater contribution to my company due to my increased engagement. I couldn't expect my bosses to know what I loved to do and I couldn't expect others to make me more engaged. I had to do this myself.

A key ingredient of strength is energy because we are doing what we enjoy and do best. My strengths kept me energised, purposeful and lively throughout the day. As long as I could help one person at work each day, I felt fulfilled and satisfied. Previously difficult and annoying tasks didn't seem as difficult or annoying any more.

In the past, I would feel depleted every day and barely could manage anything other than my job and my kids, I was now able to manage a job, degree, kids and volunteering and still felt energetic. This was opposite to everything I had experienced about study and work to date. I had become accustomed to motivate myself with affirmations, chocolate and coffee. I had been so used to pushing myself through each day with sheer determination and willpower. I now found myself with almost infinite energy at the end of each day.

My confidence lifted significantly, too. Although I still didn't understand the technical side of things, this no longer bothered me as I could see the value I added to others. The energy and joy I received from being in touch with my unique strengths made my heart full and I became more accepting of others and myself. My renewed energy and passion helped me thrive in every area of life and attracted right opportunities that aligned with my natural talents. I was offered roles that were aligned with my strengths although I had almost zero experience on the paper: a leadership coach role for one company, a strategy consulting director for another.

Since the strength practice, I found my zest back. You see, strength creates clarity and clarity creates confidence.

By observing what comes to you naturally and what energises you, you will start to take control of how you work and how you live. You will bring your best and most natural strengths to everything you do, and the more you use them, the more effectively you will get things done. You will be your optimum self, no matter what situation you are in. When you combine your strengths with diligence, you will be unstoppable.

Many assume they must quit everything to pursue a satisfying career. This is what I thought, too. This is a missed opportunity. How many of us get excited when we begin a new job, then only six months later feel that familiar dreadful feeling? That is often because we haven't learned how to use our strengths.

So, challenge yourself to find creative ways to use your strengths in your current job or business. If you don't learn how to incorporate your strengths into your daily work, even when you are ready to follow your passion, it is unlikely you will make it work. In most situations, it is our ability to make the most of our strengths that leads us to a meaningful and happy career. How you get the job done is equally as important as the job itself.

Let you and your inner genius take the driver seat

We all have a vision for ourselves, I have found most people are able to articulate what they want to do but they don't believe they can. Not realizing it's their own mindset standing in their way, they spend energy in searching for that "perfect" thing only to face the same fear over and over.

Fear can be conquered because it stems from the person you once were, not the person you are becoming. We have a fear of failure because we think failure is final and represents us personally. In fact, it's not the failure that scares us, it's how we view failure.

When my younger daughter Angie was eight years old, she lost in her gymnastic district competition. Until then, she had been accustomed to winning in her local competitions. She put on a brave face for her coach and teammates, but I could tell she was crushed. When we got into the car, she burst into tears. She had never tasted failure until now. I told her I was proud of her no matter what. Despite my encouragement, she said she wasn't sure whether she should continue gymnastics. She doubted if she was good enough for it.

We never entered her into gymnastics to win anything. We chose it because she loved it and couldn't stop doing handstands and tumbling every day. But failure can scare us and dampen our enthusiasm. I told her if she truly disliked gymnastics, she could stop doing it. But if she still loved it, it would be a pity to let one competition stop her from doing something she enjoyed.

Many people never try things again after one failure. Getting up again after having failed took enormous courage, but Angie continued with her gymnastics. She enjoyed her training and won a medal in the state championship a few months later. It's not winning a medal at a larger competition that mattered. What mattered was that she had not confused failure with who she was as a person like I did for 25 years after my first failure at school with physics. She learned that failure and winning were both parts of life.

Nobody wants to fail deliberately but knowing failure is part of growth normalises it. Instead of viewing it as an external validation of self-worth, you can look at each failure situationally and objectively, learn from it and use it as a springboard for something greater.

Everything has an expiry date, including your self-limiting beliefs and fear. It's up to you to decide on that date: let go and acknowledge it was an outdated and inaccurate assumption.

Elizabeth Gilbert, author of *Big Magic* has a ritual before she began any project, she would say, *"Hi, fear. You can come along for the ride, but you will sit in the back seat, and you will not make any decision. I and my creative genius are going to make the decisions on this journey ahead."*

Your old beliefs may still creep up on you from time to time but knowing they are no longer valid; they are old rotten beliefs that you can throw away and sit at the back seat means they lose their power. Ultimately, it's you, and your inner genius are going to take the driver seat on the journey ahead.

Reflection

- What might be a long-held negative belief for you?
- What evidence do you have to prove your negative belief is wrong?

Daily Practice

To strengthen the More Strength practice, you can simply ask yourself this one question:
- What was one natural strength I enjoyed using today?

At end of each day, you can also reflect quietly how you went today:
- What joy did I notice when I use one of my strengths?
- How much more productive did I become when I use my strengths?
- What creative way did I come up with today to use more of my strengths?

6
Do Less

> *The difference between successful people and
> really successful people is that really successful
> people say no to almost everything.*
> WARREN BUFFET

Do you believe that even if everything in your life was perfect, but if you are always tired from working, you actually will rarely feel happy? This may sound straightforward on the surface, yet so many of us overlook the direct relationship between our body and our mind. The truth is when our body is not performing well, it is unlikely we can feel well at an emotional level.

A 2017 research from Australian National University shows that working longer than 39 hours a week puts your health at risk if you also spend more than 28 hours a week in caring or domestic work (the median in Australia). These people will more likely experience mental illness and symptoms of distress such as feeling nervous, anxious or down. Given many professionals and business owners work more than 50 hours a week, what this tells us is working more is not the answer; we need to work smarter.

It's counter-intuitive to think slowing down helps you go faster. Elite sports people have mastered this approach. It is no wonder that the world of coaching and peak performance originated from the sports field. The top players are as serious about restoration as they do training. The faster they know how to recover and renew themselves, the faster and more consistently they reach their peak state. Like a car, we need to be serviced regularly if we want to stay in top shape. Often, doing less can achieve more.

In this chapter, you will learn how to create a success habit by doing less and achieving more. Essentially, doing less is about being in tune with your physical and mental wellbeing and knowing how and when to take care of both. By learning how to work at an optimal level, you will achieve a whole new level of productivity, mental agility, and wellness.

The myth of working hard

The notion that success comes from more work, not less, is hard-wired into our collective system. There are many stories of hard-working people succeeding after years of effort: sporting legends, entrepreneurs, inventors and leaders we admire. We learn that whoever works the hardest and longest wins.

I didn't need to look far to find my own stories of this idea in action. As a child, I watched my father work until 3am every day after a day's teaching. My parents proudly told me this was why he became the youngest professor in his university, despite not starting university until the age of 28. His gifts and passion for mathematics were never mentioned. In fact, my father would regularly say he was not that smart. I realised later, he was just being humble and teaching me to have a good work ethic. But in a young child's mind, the message I heard was, "Work hard and you can do anything." I always believed pushing myself was a good trait, a sign of my mental and physical strength.

In my 20-plus-years corporate career, I witnessed first-hand a culture of excessive work hours, especially amongst the high achievers. They were proud of their ability to pull an all-nighter and still turn up the next day, present with clarity and energy. Parents routinely started their second shift after putting their kids to bed. They could travel across time zones, completely jet lagged yet able to sit through back-to-back meetings with almost no rest and still able to go to events at night appearing sharp. It was hard-core and I was one of them. Privately, we desperately wanted a break, yet we pushed on, proud of our toughness and discipline.

Sacrifice is inherent to the idea of being a winner. Growing up in China, we learned many Chinese proverbs and famous stories about self-sacrifice. To motivate us to work harder, our teachers often told us the legend of Sūn Jìng from the Han Dynasty. Sūn Jìng studied late into the night and he couldn't help but doze off occasionally. To stay awake, he tied one end of a rope to his hair and the other end to a roof beam. When he fell asleep at his desk, the rope would tug his hair as his head drooped downwards. The pain woke him so he could continue studying. Over years of continuous hard work, he eventually became a renowned scholar.

Even if you didn't share my upbringing, you can probably relate to this. No pain, no gain is a common mantra for high achievers. During my time in corporate, I never heard anybody suggest we make things easier. Every project, every goal, every target was positioned as highly challenging, sometimes almost impossible to achieve. It was admirable when we declared, "This is going to be tough but we can do it." Leaders motivated their teams by telling them to toughen up and work harder, to conquer the impossible. This is what made you *a winner*.

The emphasis is on our determination and willpower rather than whether we could actually achieve the goal. Instead of making each day better, organisations ask you to work extra hard to get that annual bonus and a few days' rest. We work to eventually get away from work.

In reality, this is counter-productive. Human beings cannot sustain a never-ending struggle. It might work for the short-term but if conquering the impossible is expected again and again, eventually people will break. Like a fuel tank, our willpower and energy need to be topped up or they will run out.

It can't be nice to wake up each day and think, "I have another day of struggle and conquering the impossible ahead."

Workaholism is a label people seldom want to wear publicly, yet secretly we often feel it represents "strength." Until, of course, this way of working starts to wreck our body. That is because many people use unhealthy means to recover themselves and do not understand how to achieve optimal performance on a daily basis.

In addition to stress, research also shows people working long hours are more likely to have a stroke and heart diseases, according to an analysis of more than half a million individuals around the world. The risk increases by as high as a third in individuals who work more than 55 hours a week compared with individuals who work 9-5.

There is a limit to how hard we can work – working against our natural rhythm eventually leads to damage. When I was 20 years old, I worked such gruelling hours in my first management position in Shanghai, half my hair turned white from the stress. I hoped I could lead a more balanced life in Sydney, but 12 years later, the same attitude of hard work led to my life-threatening infection. I was a healthy eater and did not drink or smoke. My only vices were one or two cups of coffee a day and some chocolate. Yet the stress, disruptive working patterns and my lack of knowledge on wellbeing wrecked my body and led me to my illness.

Your happiness has a direct impact on the people around you, so taking care of yourself should always be a priority. If you're not looking after yourself, you can't look after others. We sometimes feel guilty for taking time to put our needs first, but not looking after ourselves is ultimately more selfish.

Understanding peak performance

Research on productivity shows that working more hours doesn't necessarily equate to better performance. Professor John Pencavel from Stanford University found in his studies that employee output falls sharply after 50 working hours per week, and falls off a cliff after 55 hours, and someone who puts in 70 hours produces nothing more with those extra 15 hours.

Since I learned this principle, I reduced my working hours significantly. I challenged myself to deliver the same or greater outcomes by working within certain hours rather than all day and all night.

One strategy I use is to simply limit my working hours. I have a hard stop every day and it varies depending on the day. Over time, you will know your pattern if you pay attention to it. For instance, it might be 4pm on Tuesday so you can pick up the kids, 8pm on Wednesdays due to mandatory conference calls and 3pm on Fridays to wind down for the weekend. I was more accommodating when I worked in corporate as I managed multiple countries, but now I run my own business, so I have a hard stop at 5pm every day and 3pm on Friday most weeks. I worked long hours in my first year of setting up business, I had since tried to reduce my working hours each year.

There is no rule. Be flexible and don't compare. The point is, by setting a target for yourself, it forces you to prioritise your energy and manage your time differently.

A limitation on your time drives you to devise ways to work more efficiently. You learn to focus wholly on the task at hand and not be distracted by emails or unrelated interruptions. A clear example of this is working mothers. Women often become more efficient after having children out of necessity, as their available hours are reduced.

Optimise your energy level

Have you ever felt that two hours of good work is better than 20 hours of poor work? Or have you spent hours trying to figure out something to no avail, yet you were able to solve the problem in 10 minutes the next morning? It's likely that you were rested and energised to do the work.

If you feel less motivated to do something you were previously excited about, it might be an indication that your energy is running low and it's time to rest and renew. Instead of blaming yourself for lacking perseverance, take a break, then come back to see whether your mood and energy level have changed.

Once we understand how to work with our energy level, it is incredible how we can do less yet achieve more. Research on peak performance shows the more we understand how to renew our energy, the more productive we become. We all have optimal periods when we are naturally more productive. Clinical psychologist Dr Michael Breus suggests in his groundbreaking book *The Power of When* that we each have different energy cycles throughout the day, the key is to make minor changes to align our routine with our natural rhythm.

For most of us, our energy level tends to be highest in the morning. It starts to fade as the day goes on, so you might consider doing your more cognitively taxing work in the morning and the less difficult tasks later in the day to make the most of your peak performance zones.

Morning is also when we have the most clarity and strongest willpower so that you could turn mornings into your productive heaven. I know many people have the intent to work on a passion project or a side venture, but they regularly put them off because they feel exhausted by the time they finish a day of work and caring the family, so often, I suggest they switch the routine instead of pushing themselves to work harder. What they have found is that they could dive into the tasks much easier in the morning.

I often feel my willingness to work on tasks wanes as the afternoon rolls on, yet I wake up in the morning motivated to keep going. So, instead of pushing through in the evenings, I rest and am always able to complete the task in one-third of the time or even shorter the next morning. Of course, if you feel most energetic in the afternoons or evenings, you need to adjust the routines to suit your own energy cycles. But overall, research shows that self-control is a finite source, so we start to lose the willpower as the day goes on.

Reflection

- Do you notice the different energy level in you throughout the day?
- If not, how can you start noticing more?

Restore your energy daily

Being more aware of our daily energy enables us to tune ourselves regularly. Instead of letting your energy go up and down and relying on external stimulation such as coffee, sugar, and high energy drink, it is better to keep your body at an optimal state throughout the day.

One way to restore our energy every day is to take regular breaks instead of resting on the weekends only or worse, relying on annual holidays. Daily restoration re-energises you so you come back quicker and faster. Plan your activities and tasks around your energy levels throughout the day.

I used to feel guilty for resting. Now I know taking a break helps my performance. Feeling energised is vital for me to perform better, so I have learned to actively build breaks into my daily rhythm.

In the past, if I did something during working hours, it needed to be relevant to my work. Now, I realise doing anything that makes me laugh or appreciate life instantly improves my energy levels. Whenever I am tired at work, instead of pushing through, I find ways to restore myself. I will have my favourite tea, go for a walk, sit in the sun, nap or meditate. Anything to do with nature and nourishing the body helps us renew quickly. On that front, checking social media for hours does not provide the restoration our bodies need as it further stimulates the brain.

My friend Nicola told me that since she started taking her puppy for walks, she started to generate great ideas every day. Her creativity was sparked to such a degree that after a few months, she started to write a play – something she had been passionate about for a long time but had never got around doing. By simply taking 20 minutes to do something that brought her joy and a mental break, she gave herself the space to slow down and be more present and creative. Research supports this, walking in nature refreshes us, improves our mood, and increases our cognitive performance.

I'm not suggesting we all rush out and get a puppy. The lesson here is that on the surface, some activities seem leisurely and non-productive, when in fact, they provide vital recovery time. Your ability to renew yourself by monitoring your energy and restoring it naturally is key to greater performance, happiness and wellbeing.

Reflection

- What can you do to restore your energy more often?

Design vs. React: Take control of your daily agenda

We often feel overwhelmed and paralysed because we believe we have no control over our daily lives. When we let tasks and meetings overtake us, we feel lost. This impacts our mood, productivity and wellbeing. The most significant step we can take is to regain a sense of control. We can decide how we spend our time. After all, it's our time. Instead of reacting to other people's demands, we can take control of our day. If we don't determine how we spend our time, other people will. When we lose control in one aspect of our lives, it spills over into others.

Most people go through life reacting. Very few proactively design their life. How much of your time is spent reacting to what people say in meetings or emails? With the number of emails most people receive every day, it's a wonder anyone can get anything done at all. As Seth Godin, author of *Purple Cow* says, In fact, many of us are stuck in a perpetual cycle of reacting and responding instead of innovating and initiating.

Most of us are great responders but we go home never doing anything we had wanted to do. It is possible to spend our entire life responding. Looking back at my two CMO jobs, the biggest difference was I took ownership of the way I worked in my second role. I started to initiate more.

Because as much as I seemed to be achieving in my first CMO role, I simply let things happen to me. I achieved by working very hard. If you had asked me what I would have liked to do, I could have told you. But I also would have added that those things would have to wait until I had done all the things I had to do, and that could mean in a long time or never. I was the master of getting through, multitasking and managing a huge volume of incoming demands, and I was proud of it. But I was miserable. I had no capacity or time to do anything I wanted to do. How can you not be miserable if you can't ever do your own things?

Think for a second – from the moment you got up today, how many things did you do that you wanted to do (proactive)? How many of those things were you simply reacting (reactive)? If you didn't do many proactive things, why? If most of your hours are spent reacting, you're likely to feel exhausted and out of control.

Most of my clients are professionals, executives and entrepreneurs who are not bound by exact hours. They don't have to work or sit at their designated desk every hour, they have a degree of autonomy. But most of them go to work reacting, not proactively taking control of the situation.

Constantly checking email is a typical mistake people make. With a few exceptions, most of us do not need to check and respond to emails the minute we wake up. As Greg McKeown says in his book *Essentialism*, if you don't prioritise yourself, somebody else will.

Researchers from the University of Leipzig have found that morning people are more proactive than evening types; meaning they have a stronger willingness and ability to take actions. Rising early and having a routine therefore is a great way to set yourself up for success each day. Instead of reacting, always plan your day with the things you want to achieve first, then evaluate how many other things you can achieve realistically.

It's important to stick to your plan, even for just 30-60 minutes at the beginning of the day before throwing yourself into reactive mode. I used to be a night owl; spent my day in putting fire out and then tried to work on the things I wanted to do after putting the kids to bed. It was exhausting and ineffective. I learned to start my day early, and with tasks I like to accomplish. I plan this the night before and revisit that list before I start the day in the morning. Everything else can wait until I have decided what my goals are for the day. I work far less hours yet 3-4 times more productive.

Over time, you can build a success habit of putting essential tasks ahead of non-essential tasks. Essential does not mean every task that comes your way and lands in your inbox or on your desk. Essential means the most important things you want to accomplish that day.

Life is not perfect. We all must do some non-essential tasks. However, designing your day around the most important goals will naturally give you a mental boost. You will feel more accomplished and productive. You will be able to clearly see the things that can wait or simply not happen at all.

Reflection

- What one change can you make so you can have more control of your day?

Hesitate before saying yes

Doing less and achieving more requires you to be clear about your priorities. One of the major challenges is being more selective about the things you say yes to. You can only do one thing at a time, so saying yes to one thing effectively means you are saying no to something else. Are you happy to miss out on something else?

Saying yes to every request sends the wrong message about your true expertise and value. It's more helpful to everyone to say no sometimes and refer the opportunity to someone who would value it more. That way, you are available to say yes to the things you truly value.

I used to be a yes person, a people-pleaser. I remember I was praised for saying yes faster than anybody else. "What great feedback," I thought. "It shows I'm eager, I'm capable, I'm committed, right?" No. It showed I had no awareness of my priorities and didn't value my time.

Now I consider what saying yes means. I hesitate before saying yes and base my decision to say yes on my own set of value questions:

- Is this valuable?
- Is this necessary?
- Will I add value?

- Am I the best person to do it?
- What do I need to say no to in order to do this?
- Can this be delegated or outsourced?
- Will I enjoy it?
- Does this even need to be looked at?
- What if I say no?

Eliminate distractions to restore your mind

With the increased usage of technology, our ability to concentrate is declining, yet it is critical to our success. Dr Cal Newport from Georgetown University has shared extensive research in his book *Deep Work* to show why the ability to focus and do deep work is one thing that will give information age workers a huge advantage.

Bill Gates, the founder of Microsoft, spends one week alone, twice a year in a forest. He calls his ritual the "Think Week." Gates came up with this idea as a way to innovate and think creatively. Tucked away in his secret cabin, Gates spends the week ponding on new ideas, away from distractions in day-to-day life – alone with his own thoughts and dozens of papers. In a rare interview with Robert GuthStaff, a journalist from *Wall Street Journal*, Gates shared that these weeks tend to include a lot of reading and a lot of thinking. It's been said that one Think Week in 1995 inspired his famous, "The Internet Tidal Wave" paper, while another prompted Gates to come up with the plans for Microsoft's Tablet PC.

I often encourage my clients to block at least one hour on their working calendar each day to focus on the things most important to them. When others see your calendar is blocked for that hour, they will find another time to work with you. You need that hour to do the most meaningful things, things that require zero interruptions and distractions. You might still have to attend meetings occasionally during that time, but the fact that hour is in your calendar serves as a daily reminder. Gradually, you learn to block half days and even whole days to work on strategic and innovative projects.

Changing habits requires an open mind

Most people don't think they can change their situation unless they get rid of it entirely. However, if you don't have an open mind, it is unlikely you have the courage to change the entire situation. And even if you do, it's likely you haven't learned good habits to manage future situations better.

People often leave corporate to pursue personal freedom only find themselves working even harder as their own boss. They have carried this unhealthy habit with them and made it worse without the support of teams.

People often say, "This is just the way my job or my business is, it's not possible to change." What I have discovered is that they often haven't even tried anything new, they have simply allowed their old habits to continue and have convinced themselves it is the reality.

There are many simple techniques that can help us do less and achieve more. For example, switching tasks requires enormous energy as we redirect our focus and recall information. Research shows we lose up to 40% efficiency when we switch tasks regularly. It disturbs our productivity and flow. Therefore, productivity experts advise we set aside time to deal with emails in blocks rather than respond to them instantly. Whenever I share this data with my clients, they are able to manage emails in a much more efficient way and can often save 2-3 hours per day by adopting this one simple new habit.

No matter how many tasks and demands we are given, we ultimately have control over how we manage them. We can decide how we react to them and how we do things in a way that makes us happier and more productive. All it takes is an open and agile mind. What small changes can I make today? Maybe instead of meeting people sitting down, you could have a walking meeting, for example. By taking even the tiniest of steps, you demonstrate to yourself you do have control.

Everything can be redesigned if you are willing and open and there are many amazing ways you can improve your efficiency. If you have the freedom to work from home, you can work from a café or even the beach once a week to break the monotony. Neuroscience shows that our brain gains new insights from new environments. In fact, research has shown that a moderate level of ambient noise created by places such as coffee shops improves our concentration and creativity. Even if you work in an office, you can still work from a café for a couple of hours. At my last workplace, Adobe, my colleagues and I regularly worked from the staff kitchen or downstairs food court. Admittedly, we had a nice kitchen and food court.

Some jobs are harder to be re-designed. I acknowledge that, I have been there. Most jobs, however, can be. You might not be able to redesign it to perfection, but it can be redesigned to suit your strengths and enhance your productivity if you are willing to take ownership of it.

Sometimes the person who complains the most about their

workload is the person who allows others to invade their private hours with open arms. Often, they choose to answer emails at all hours. I did it myself in my early years, until one day I could no longer cope with the volume of work. My manager told me he would give me more headcount once I had figured out how to work more efficiently. I was angry with him but he was right. My eagerness to please and insecurity created many unnecessary late nights for myself.

Start with what matters to you

I remember feeling resentful having to travel overseas for work on my birthday one year, sitting at an airport terminal at 2am in KL, Malaysia, waiting to be transited to another city. When I eventually told my manager about my resentment, he said, "Why didn't you tell me earlier? I would never have asked you to travel had I known it was your birthday." Since then, I have never travelled for work on any occasions that matter to me.

What are the non-negotiable things in your life? Put them in your diary and plan around them. Be clear with others and yourself that these things are important and cannot be moved at the last minute. Most people value honesty and transparency.

What are the things you want to do the most? Can you achieve them first? The answer is yes, regardless of whether you work for somebody or work for yourself. It takes awareness, proactive planning and constant adjustment. Put yourself in the driver's seat – don't let life just happen to you.

What are three things you would like to accomplish today so you will feel good? We all have at least one.

One of my best friends is the *delete* button. Instead of adding things to my list, every morning I ask myself what I can delete. When we don't learn to change our daily agenda and actions, it's not possible to have a different outcome.

You decide how you run your day. You decide what matters and what doesn't. Knowing you are in control is powerful. As leadership expert John Maxwell says in his book, *Make Today Count*, "The secret of your success is determined by your daily agenda."

....

Reflection

- What one habit you would like to implement starting from today?

....

Daily Practice

To strengthen the Do Less practice, you can simply ask yourself this one question:
- What have I done less of today to enable me to achieve more?

At the end of each day, you can also reflect quietly how you went today:
- Have I aligned my tasks with my energy level?
- Did I feel better and work more productively after taking breaks?
- What creative way did I come up with today to do less and achieve more?

7
More Passion

Don't ask yourself what the world needs. Ask yourself what makes you come alive, and go do that, because what the world needs is people who have come alive.
HOWARD THURMAN

There is a well-known Chinese proverb that says, "Choose a job you love and you will never have to work a day in your life." The search for that one perfect job – what I was born to do, so every day would be fun and fulfilling – consumed me for a long time.

I followed every hobby and fleeting interest to see if I could discover my calling. I started numerous courses and invested in all the necessary books. What I discovered while pursuing so many different avenues wasn't a waste of time. I learned that there are many things that can inspire us and allow us to use our gifts. One job couldn't possibly express them all. I realised my work could never define me because there was so much more to me than my job.

Many people try to understand their strengths and passions so they can find their career and business direction. What they often fail to do is incorporate these strengths and passions into their day-to-day life.

Humans need novelty and creativity instead of stagnation. This is not a greedy desire; it is a natural human need that allows us to grow and thrive. Most of us tend to get repetition at work and this impacts our motivation, confidence and drive. However, we can create the novelty and growth experience outside work. Bringing your passion and gifts into your life beyond treating them as a way to find a career path or a business idea will bring you renewed energy. And gradually, through this practice, it is possible to combine passion with living.

I used to believe I had to wait to pursue my passions until after my corporate career ended. There would be time for them later in life. This thinking held me back from learning to enjoy each day to the fullest. I now believe this is an excuse – your job shouldn't stop you from experiencing passion in your life today!

Joy brings meaning and success

Dr Emma Seppala, Standford University researcher and professor in the field of happiness, found that happiness was not the result of achievement; rather, it was the precursor of any sustainable success.

I always thought joy and achievement could not co- exist. I valued achievement over joy. I had spent my entire life achieving without joy. My hope was that by staying focused on success, I would get the happiness I deserved. I never thought it was the other way around. Joy is a pre-requisite for great performance and results. By focusing on finding joy and meaning in every day and moment, we achieve things more easily.

I discovered this principle almost by accident. When I was working in my second CMO role, I had started to volunteer as a board member for the Australia Computer Society. As part of my volunteer commitment, I organised several industry events a year. One of the events was aimed at women and the theme was strengths. We expected to get 50 attendees. We had 400 people register for the event! The response was overwhelming after the event as well.

This was another defining moment in my life. I realised I was doing something that made a difference. It was incredibly satisfying. I also realised I could achieve the goals that were aligned with my purpose while working in a job I might not be born to do.

Over the following months, I continued with my volunteer work both inside and outside organisations, creating more learning events for the industry and mentoring people during my spare time. Opportunities kept coming – a panelist for roundtable discussions, speaker opportunities, interview opportunities. I hosted several larger events and was even invited to speak at an event overseas.

The more I gave, the more I received. I was simply doing what brought me joy and satisfaction. I had thought quitting my executive job was the only way to find my purpose, yet there I was, with the opportunity to do both in my hands.

When I stopped using my job as a reason for not doing what I loved, I discovered something else: my job doesn't represent everything I am. I am more. I also realised that I could find meaning in my job. Why did I think all I had to do every day was turn up to work in my role only? I realised I was bigger than my role. I realised I had made myself small. I no longer wanted to be small. I had the perfect opportunity to influence and contribute in a greater capacity than what my job required.

I was no longer someone who was trapped by a job. I chose not to be defined by my job and became fully aware my job was only a fraction of my professional identity.

I no longer viewed myself with a designated position, expected to turn up every day on autopilot, restricted to performing only a few tasks. I am a person. I am not a job or an accumulation of tasks. It's up to me how I work and how I deliver the best outcome.

We humans derive meaning from serving others and making contributions. We can be purposeful even when we are not in an ideal job. Some people are lucky to have a job that allows them to express many of their talents. For most people, that's not the case. However, we each have enormous potential and gifts to share every day. I advise my clients to view their day job as only part of their professional endeavour. We need to take the ownership to find projects within or outside work to express your passion and talents and create meaningful experiences.

Gradually, you will work towards a career, business or calling that will represent as many of your talents as possible. More often than not, a job or calling requires a collection of roles, not just one role. Today, I have found my calling, and I am expressing it in a variety of my roles as a coach, mentor, speaker, and writer, I have a feeling that I will continuously evolve every year.

When our work is meaningful for others and ourselves, it gives us immense satisfaction and drives us to even more meaningful work.

....

Reflection

- When did you do something you enjoyed without thinking about the outcome, and it brought you a positive result anyway?

....

Joy is a greater way of achieving

In her *New York Times* bestseller, *Big Magic*, Elizabeth Gilbert says there are many writers who want to write so they can become famous. To Gilbert, they are missing the point. She writes because she loves writing and it brings her joy, whether she gets published or not. This means she can write freely and consistently every day. Instead of focusing on the prize, she focuses on her joy and intrinsic motivation to do her best work every day. Her prize? Four *New York Times* bestsellers within 10 years.

It's not one thing that makes us happy, it's doing things that bring us joy and meaning every day that make us happy. We all thrive on motion and energy.

When I decided to study my Master of Coaching Psychology, I was working in my second Chief Marketing Officer role while raising my two daughters. Psychology was not an easy subject for me to learn. It had many big words and my English wasn't good enough, so I had to use a dictionary to aid my study. But I enjoyed it so much that I achieved a great result in an exceptionally short period of time.

I had not done well with studying since I failed physics when I was 10 years old. I had constantly battled with self-doubt. But because I felt naturally motivated, studying psychology was not a chore or an additional task – it energised me. I hadn't felt that energised for a long time. Being happy dramatically improved my health, my productivity at work and my mood as a tired mother. I learned something profound about human motivation from this: enjoyment creates greater results. Putting yourself into a state of joy is the key to sustainable performance, happiness and success. *Joy became my new way of achieving, a more natural way of achieving.*

Moments of joy are necessary for the human spirit

I used to view moments of joy as a luxury. Doing anything for leisure was something I deserved only after I had worked hard. Then I realised joy was not a mere reward for hard work, but a necessity for our soul.

As children, we naturally knew how to play and create fun experiences. As we get older, we start to lose the ability to have fun. George Bernard Shaw famously said: *We don't stop playing because we grow old; we grow old because we stop playing.* However, research has shown that having fun reduces stress, improves our relationship, keeps us energetic, and increases more job satisfaction.

Have you ever had a delicious breakfast and felt immediately better about the day ahead? Compared to, say, a day when you rushed out of home and chewed on your dry muesli bar on the way to work? Why? Nutrition aside, when you have a great breakfast, you create a beautiful experience to begin your day.

In the morning, I sometimes sit on my veranda and watch the sunrise with my cup of tea. It might only take a few minutes but it immediately fills me with joy and gratitude and I feel ready to embrace the day ahead. When I play with my dog silly at the park, I always walk home feeling much more energetic and joyful. What fun activities do you enjoy doing?

Our state of mind needs to be constantly managed for our body and mind to be at an optimal level at all times. You will produce better work and be happier at the same time. So, don't wait. Whatever you can do now to improve your state, start there.

Fill your day with joyful moments

Every day, we have thousands of moments to either put ourselves in a satisfying, positive state of mind or a dissatisfying, negative state. Many of these moments are within our control. How you manage each moment of your day is important. I like to start my day with what I enjoy. If you have the freedom to work from home, you can work from a nice café or the beach once a week. Instead of rewarding yourself afterwards, mindfully set yourself up for success from the beginning.

You don't need to wait for joy to happen. Joy can be created. We can all create happy moments through simple strategies and daily habits. Whenever I feel my mood decline, nine out of 10 times it is because I'm overworked. So, I gently ask myself, "What could I do now to bring some energy back? How can I make it more joyful?"

It could be a gentle walk, calling a friend, spending time with your loved ones – anything that reminds us life is meant to be enjoyed. Even when you have a deadline looming or are in a stressful situation, nothing should stop you from experiencing these joyful moments and feeling you have had a good day.

You shouldn't need to wait to have these moments until you have reached a major milestone, either – such as a big new client, promotion or meeting a huge deadline. You can celebrate moments of joy today and every day. These moments remind you why you do what you do. They make what you do feel worthwhile and meaningful. They sustain you and give you a sense of purpose.

....

Reflection

- How can you bring more fun and joyful moments into your day-to-day life?

....

Connect with your lost passion and embrace passion projects

Letting go of an important, serious job to pursue a creative passion is not a practical choice for most of us who have financial responsibilities. But why does it have to be one way or the other? We can keep our jobs or businesses while connecting with our passions – just in a smaller way to balance them well.

Write down your list of passions, like this:
- I love helping others with their career and life
- I am interested in human psychology, self-development and

growth
- I like writing
- I like motivating teams and individuals
- I like photography

Create time to experiment with each. Not all at the same time. Start with the easiest option so you can start incorporating your passions into your day-to-day life straight away.

Your passions only need a little investment to stay alive. Carve out 30-60 minutes a day and just start, whether by writing notes in a journal or reflecting on the train, listening to a podcast or researching – it all counts. Do you like mentoring? Start mentoring. Do you enjoy bringing people together? Do it, even just once a month.

You don't have to wait until you have paid off the mortgage and your kids are older. It takes time to build anything, so why not use that time to practise your craft? Instead of thinking it's extra work to do, think of it as creating an *energy source* that will help you thrive at work and in life. Doing something you love will make you much happier. Even if what you do is on a small scale, it's better than nothing and will help boost your confidence. Each year you delay pursuing your passions, it will take longer to build your courage and confidence.

We all have lost dreams. I wanted to be a writer. But the fear of living in poverty and disappointing my parents got in the way of my passion. So, I chose to follow what I thought was the safer option – a corporate career. I told myself I could write any time. Gradually, the inner voice inspiring me to write was silenced, and my soul died a little. After I learned how important it is to keep our passion going without worrying about whether it leads to a financial outcome or not,

I started to re-connect with writing just for fun. I felt immediately alive just after writing one blog. One of my clients Kate said to me one day connecting with the passion will revive you, it's like having a new lease on life.

Exploring your passions will open up your heart and make you a happier person, which will also benefit the people around you. You will no longer feel you are so restricted as you are expressing your whole self in a meaningful way. *Instead of work towards happiness, learn to follow what brings you the joy.*

Calling

I used to think I had to choose between a career and a calling. I also thought my life wouldn't be purposeful enough until I found that calling.

Truth be told, even our calling changes. We evolve even after we have found our purpose. We are complex beings, it's not possible to know everything about ourselves in a single year, through a single retreat or even multiple retreats and vision exercises. I find not knowing everything keeps life fresh and exciting. I am curious about what life unfolds. It means we are always ready to embrace new opportunities.

Most people like discovering their purpose through thinking. I have found a much better and faster way is through doing it. Through doing purposeful work and embracing your passion, you will naturally discover more purpose and passion.

People who end up working in their calling often don't start with absolute clarity. They usually start with something small. You want to help the world? Start helping one person today. This gives you the skill, experience, evidence and confidence to keep going.

You want to run a business? Start sharing that idea now, don't wait until you quit your job. You want to coach somebody full time one day? Help a colleague today by using some coaching techniques and see how you go. You want to write a book? Start writing blog posts. You want to be a chef? Start cooking for people and designing your own menu.

Do you know what kind of activities make you excited and satisfied? These are activities you do purely for enjoyment. You can find these examples, right? Instead of dreaming about what might be your dream job, start investing time in observing, discovering and harnessing what brings you joy.

Sense of joy will guide you naturally and effortlessly to the things you love.

Fuzzy vision is enough – don't let perfectionism stop you

One thing that holds most people back from change is the need to feel 100% ready and have a perfect plan to go. They need to dream, think, plan and achieve a sense of readiness. Then it needs to be "the right time".

We all know the feeling of 100% preparedness never comes.

I used to think I had to know where I was headed before I took action. I also believed I could only do what I love after I found that one "perfect" thing. However, *real clarity comes from experimenting*. We often don't know whether we really like something until we give it a try. Life is a box of experiment. The perfect plan is always a result of frequent imperfect actions and adjustments.

Trial and experiment are all part of the learning process. To avoid the learning process is to avoid real success. At one stage in my life, I toyed with so many ideas over so many years that I could honestly end up winning a Guinness Record for ideas. It was frustrating, to say the least because none of my thoughts ever came to light. I became a great thinker, but a terrible doer.

Ideas come and go; the ability to do something about it is a far more important skill to master, to be able to do that gives you total freedom in life, so you never feel restricted that you must come up with one idea, one perfect plan. You can be successful in many ways.

So nowadays, whenever I see myself hesitate in embracing a great idea, I pause. Instead of going back to the same pattern hoping for a perfect plan, I ask myself the question – Is it my idea that needs more work or do I need more work to strengthen my experimental mindset.

When we have this mentality, we will no longer be overwhelmed, because we know that we can be flexible in our endeavours, nothing is final, we learn to embrace the art of experimentation. One thing I learned from working for software industry is that all the great companies constantly launch imperfect products. They then make revision almost every day after the launch. It is only through listening to the customer feedback and making the ongoing adjustments, they were able to create great products.

Dr Anthony Grant introduces the concept of fuzzy vision in his book, *Coach Yourself*. This concept has changed the way I view planning. Planning is something fun, not something you have to get perfect. We all want a plan so we know where we are going and don't waste our energy. The problem is, we try to perfect the plan and take too long. Start with a rough outline and get feedback. Practising your craft takes time – don't wait until everything is lined up.

Start now and once you have created action, motion and energy, you will be surprised how many opportunities will start coming your way. If you learn to act today instead of sitting there, waiting for absolute clarity to fall from the sky, you can make almost any positive change.

Just start – One step at a time

I am sure we can all think of a change we have wanted to make for a long time, yet we haven't had the courage to do it. Why? Often it's because the steps to get there seem so difficult, we procrastinate and feel scared.

Successful change requires small, achievable steps, so simple and easy that you can just give them a go. This is the best way to manage change. It reduces fear and uncertainty, provides you with real-time feedback, and gives you the confidence you need to continue.

In her book, *Bird by Bird,* Anne Lamott, explains the best way to write is to start by filling a one-inch frame. Her point is that we often become so obsessed with creating the right action from the first go, we struggle to do anything at all. Instead, we should simply start by concentrating on the smallest action we can make. This one, tiny action will lead to another and another. A writer doesn't start by thinking about writing a bestseller. They start by writing and filling that first small frame.

Don't make it so hard you can't even start. Don't throw away everything to pursue your "perfect" vision. All we need to do is take some tiny steps to get it started. These tiny steps have more impact than a gigantic idea that never sees the light of day. Ignoring the possibility of doing one small thing today means you're protecting the status quo and choosing your current situation. Choosing to act gives you the opportunity to break your unhealthy working habits and limited self-beliefs. There is a Chinese proverb that sums this up: "The best time to plant a tree is 20 years ago. The second-best time is today."

Take the example of launching a new small business. Many people imagine the process of starting a business as a dramatic, lightning-bolt experience. A genius entrepreneurial idea strikes you in an instant, you quit your corporate job and dive head-first into the new opportunity. The reality, however, is that most business owners who transition from a corporate role spend months or even years thinking, tweaking and experimenting with different ideas and models before it gets off the ground. Often, this incubation period happens while they are working in a full-time job. The new start-up could be a side hustle for a long time before they pursue the business full-time.

When I realised the need for big changes in my life, I thought I had to choose one path or the other, right there and then. The emotions I felt were unbearable. That's because I didn't understand changes happen one step at a time.

When I realised navigating change required effective strategies such as aligning my priorities with my choices, practising my strengths daily, learning about optimal performance, creating passion projects, spending less time on meaningless stuff and re-investing the time in more meaningful things, I started to pave a new path, little by little.

Over the years, I began to transition to corporate jobs that were more aligned with my strengths and passion. I also took on mentoring and speaking gigs outside my day job (some paid but mostly pro-bono), and ran projects outside and inside organisations that aligned with my purpose and were of benefit to the organisations and industry. I envisaged my new path while still working in my corporate leadership roles. My personal brand was consistent regardless of my title. Nobody was surprised when I set up my coaching practice because what I advocated in my business was what I advocated in my leadership roles.

The biggest lesson I learned was that I was able to stay present during the process. I enjoyed my corporate jobs, and I enjoy running my business today. I learned to appreciate the journey instead of counting on the destination. I learned that if I took care of today, tomorrow would be taken care of naturally.

Small daily actions won't deliver life-changing success overnight, but they will bring positive momentum and progress consistently. If you can consider your change process as a year-long experiment, you can afford to be playful and creative about it. It will be more fun and light-hearted. The more relaxed you are about this process, the more curious you are, greater outcome you will achieve.

If you make change easier, more achievable and more enjoyable, you can start now.

Reflection

- How can I make my next step so easy that I know I will definitely take action?

Daily Practice

To strengthen the More Passion practice, you can simply ask yourself this one question:

- What one enjoyable thing did I do today just for myself?

At end of each day, you can also reflect quietly how you went today:

- What moments of joy did I experience today?
- Was I being playful with trying new things today?
- What one fun activity did I do today?

PARTING WORDS
We are all on this journey together

We ask ourselves, 'Who am I to be brilliant,
gorgeous, talented, fabulous?'
Actually, who are you not to be?
MARIANNE WILLIAMSON

In my darkest moments, I felt utterly alone. I was terrified of what I would find if I opened myself up. Would I become resentful of my parents, my career, my entire life? Would there even be a solution? When I heard my friend Julia sharing her own heartache at a public event, I realised I was no longer alone. Her honesty allowed me to give myself permission to open up as well. I felt some hope in my own darkness.

Often in life, when we are consumed by our own problems, we imagine we are the only one whose whole world is tumbling down. But these problems are often shared by others and can be solved. I hope by sharing my learning and experiences, you will feel the encouragement I felt many years ago as I listened to my friend Julia's story.

The biggest lesson I learned from this journey was *self-acceptance*. You don't need to go to the ends of the earth or hide in a mountain to find yourself. You might find peace in these endeavours but your true self is right here, waiting to be noticed and heard by you.

As confusing as it was at the time, the defining moment I had so many years ago was my true self wanting to connect with me. Learning to reconnect with yourself is a beautiful thing and a beautiful journey. The more you practise this connection with your true self, the more peaceful and joyful you will become. Know that no matter how far you travel in search of happiness, it can only be found in one place.

I am eternally grateful for that moment.

DAILY PRACTICE CHECKLIST

Daily Practice – Care Less

To strengthen the Care Less practice, you can simply ask yourself this one question:
- What was one thing I cared less about today?

At end of each day, you can also reflect quietly how you went today:
- How many things did I do today just to look good?
- How many things did I do today really mattered to me?
- How many things did I do today without the concern of having to look good?

Daily Practice – More Strength

To strengthen the More Strength practice, you can simply ask yourself this one question:
- What was one natural strength I enjoyed using today?

At end of each day, you can also reflect quietly how you went today:
- What joy did I notice when I use one of my strengths?
- How much more productive did I become when I use my strengths?
- What creative way did I come up with today to use more of my strengths?

Daily Practice – Do Less

To strengthen the Do Less practice, you can simply ask yourself this one question:
- What have I done less of today to enable me to achieve more?

At end of each day, you can also reflect quietly how you went today:
- Have I aligned my tasks with my energy level?
- Did I feel better and work more productively after taking breaks?
- What creative way did I come up with today to do less and achieve more?

Daily Practice – More Passion

To strengthen the More Passion practice, you can simply ask yourself this one question
- What one enjoyable thing did I do today just for myself?

At end of each day, you can also reflect quietly how you went today:
- What moments of joy did I experience today?
- Was I being playful with trying new things today?
- What one fun activity did I do today?

NEXT STEPS

Thank you for taking the time to read this book.

If you enjoyed *Come Alive*, then you may like my blogs as well

You can sign up at: yudanshi.com

I also welcome you to join our community or participate in one of our programs

Learn more from my website: yudanshi.com

Download your complimentary workbook

I have also designed a workbook for this book. It's an additional tool to help you learn, reflect and deepen your knowledge.

You can download it from here: yudanshi.com/comealiveworkbook

Please do not hesitate to be in touch. I would be honored to hear from you and serve you in anyway.

ACKNOWLEDGEMENTS

This book is a labour of love. I am deeply grateful to everyone who has given me their support, encouragement and inspiration on this journey.

To my two amazing daughters, Jasmine and Angelique, you are the reason I wanted to live a more meaningful life. I have learned so much from watching you grow. Thank you for being my biggest supporters.

Thank you, Roslyn Richardson, for being my editor. Your wisdom and support are beyond what I ever could have hoped for. Words cannot express how thankful I am. I know I have grown leaps and bounds during the process with your guidance.

I want to thank Dr Tony Grant and Dr Suzy Green, my professors for my Master of Coaching Psychology at the University of Sydney. Dr Suzy Green, I saw you present at the Happiness & Its Cause Conference in 2009. I had never seen anybody that passionate about what they did. I knew there and then I would follow a similar path, even though I had no idea how. Dr Tony Grant, your lesson about Hollow Victory was so profound that I named the first chapter of this book after it. There are no words to describe how grateful I am for the degree you have created and the wisdom you have shared.

I want to thank all my friends at Thought Leaders. Writing a book can be daunting, but when you are surrounded by people who write while running their business, it normalises the process. Thank you, my friend Ingrid, for encouraging me to be part of the group.

I want to thank my copy editor Lauren Shay; you are so gifted in what you do. Thank you to my amazing publisher, Karen Mc Dermott, for guiding me through the post-writing process.

I also want to thank everyone who has supported my initial blog. I did not imagine the level of response I would receive as a result of sharing my journey. The comments and stories sent to me from around the world strengthened my belief that this book would benefit others.

I cannot thank all my customers enough. I wouldn't be here if it weren't for your challenges, your curiosity and your resilience. I want to thank you all for inspiring me to keep evolving.

For anybody who has appeared in my book, although I have changed your names, I think you know who you are, and I want to thank you for that influence.

Last but not least, I want to thank my parents. Thank you, Mum, for believing in me. Education was the only gateway to a better life in our circumstances, and you gave me that precious gift. Dad, I used to watch you re-write your paper 20, 30, 40 times by hand, as you didn't have a typewriter or computer. You taught me a valuable lesson: the key to doing anything well is to do it a little better each time.

REFERENCES

Chapter 1

1. **Abraham Maslow described the motivation for safety and security in his hierarchy of needs theory:** Maslow, A. H. (1943). A theory of human motivation. Psychological Review, 50(4), 370-396.

Chapter 2

2. **Research has shown our happiness doesn't necessarily increase as our income goes up:** Kahneman, D., & Deaton, A. (2010). High income improves evaluation of life but not emotional well-being, (38) 16489-16493. https:// doi.org/10.1073/pnas.1011492107

3. **Research has long shown that as we reach a certain life stage between the ages of 33-50, we start to think about the limited time we have left:** Jaques, E. (1965). Death and the mid-life crisis. The International Journal of Psychoanalysis, 46(4), 502-514

4. **Can grow a new sense of self-awareness and a higher- level of harmony and job satisfaction**: Fitzgerald, C 2002, 'Understanding and supporting the development of executives at midlife', In C. Fitzgerald & J. G. Berger (Eds.), Executive coaching: Practices and perspectives, Davies- Black Publishing, Palo Alto, CA, pp89-117

Chapter 3

5. **As James Clear observes in his book Atomic Habits, you only need 1% of improvement every day in order to achieve great results:** Clear, J. (2018). Atomic Habits: An Easy and Proven Way to Build Good Habits and Break Bad Ones.

6. **This is the art of change: our actions drive our mindset change.** Ibarra, H. (2015). Act Like a Leader, Think Like a Leader. Harvard Business Review Press

7. **Marshall Goldsmith says, "What got you here won't get you there.":** Goldsmith, M., Reiter, M. (2007). What Got You Here Won't Get You There: How Successful People Become Even More Successful (1st edition). Hyperion.

8. **Psychologists call this the "avoidance goal":** Elliot, A. J., & McGregor, H. A. (2001). A 2 × 2 achievement goal framework. Journal of Personality and Social Psychology, 80(3), 501-519.

9. **Viktor Frankl wrote his famous book, Man's Search For Meaning:** Frankl, V. E. (2006). Man's search for meaning. Boston: Beacon Press.

Chapter 4

10. **Viktor Frankl writes in his book Man's Search for Meaning, success will follow you precisely because you forget to think about it:** Frankl, V. E. (2006). Man's search for meaning. Boston: Beacon Press.

11. **In Carol Dweck's book, Mindset, she describes two different, opposing mindsets: a growth mindset and a fixed mindset:** Dweck, Carol S. **(2008) Mindset:** the new psychology of success New York: Ballantine Books

12. **Seth Godin, the author of nineteen international bestsellers says "I fail more than others":** Godin,S. (2014, February 6). If I fail more than

you do, I win. Retrieved from https://www.youtube.com/watch?v=I1Y-usP1mV0

13. **Lee said during an interview with radio host Roy Newquist in 1964:** Newquist, R. (1964). Counterpoint. Chicago: Rand Mcnally

14. **Gilbert faced the same fear as a newly celebrated author. In her 2014 Ted Talk:** Gilbert, E. (2009, February). Your elusive creative genius. Retrieved from https://www. ted.com/talks/elizabeth_gilbert_on_genius?language=en

15. **Big Magic, published in 2016:** Gilbert, E. (2015). Big magic: Creative living beyond fear. London: Bloomsbury Publishing.

16. **As J.K. Rowling, author of the Harry Potter series, famously said in her 2008 commencement speech at Harvard University:** Rowling, J.K. (2008, June 5). The fringe benefits of failure. Retrieved from https://www.ted.com/talks/jk_rowling_the_fringe_benefits_of_failure

Chapter 5

17. **In the research conducted by Jay Niblick:** Niblick, J. (2009). What's Your Genius? How The Best THINK For Success In The New Economy. St. James Publishing

18. **A global study from Corporate Leadership Council shows:** Corporate Leadership Council (2002). Building the High-Performance Workforce A Quantitative Analysis of the Effectiveness of Performance Management Strategies. Retrieved from https://docplayer.net/5496089-Building-the-high-performance-workforce-a-quantitative-analysis-of-the-effectiveness-of-performance-management-strategies.html

19. **Based on Linley, strength is a pre-existing capacity that already exists within us:** Linley, A. (2008). Average to A+: Realising Strengths in Yourself and Others. CAPP Press.

20. **Most parents think a student's lowest grades deserve the most time and attention:** Rath, T. (2013). StrengthsFinder 2.0: A New and Upgraded Edition of the Online Test from Gallup's Now Discover Your Strengths (1st edition). Gallup Press.

21. **We often let one negative experience influence how we perceive ourselves. In his book, Authentic Happiness, Martin Seligman looks at what causes people to be either pessimistic or optimistic:** Seligman, M. E. P. (2002). Authentic happiness: Using the new positive psychology to realize your potential for lasting fulfillment. New York: Free Press.

22. **We need to consciously work on developing our sense of competence:** Grant, A. & Greene, J. (2004). Coach Yourself Make Real Changes in Your Life. Pearson Education UK.

23. **Feeling competent is key to satisfying work, as Daniel Pink explains:** Pink, D. H. (2009). Drive: The surprising truth about what motivates us. New York, NY: Riverhead Books.

24. **Every time we have failed at something, been criticised or felt stupid, we have added to our negative self-talk:** Grant, A. & Greene, J. (2004). Coach Yourself Make Real Changes in Your Life. Pearson Education UK.

25. **"I and my creative genius are going to make the decisions on this journey ahead":** Gilbert, E. (2015). Big magic: Creative living beyond fear. London: Bloomsbury Publishing.

Chapter 6

26. **Researchers from Australian National University has found through a 2017 study that working longer than 39 hours a week puts your health at risk:** Medew, J. (2017, February 2). Health warning for people working more than 39 hours a week: ANU study.Retrieved from https://www.theage.com.au/national/victoria/working-more-than-39-hours-a-

week-is-bad-for-your-health-anu-study-20170202-gu45d7.html

27. **Elite sports people have mastered this approach:** Stulberg, B., & Magness, S. (2017). Peak Performance: Elevate Your Game, Avoid Burnout, and Thrive with the New Science of Success. Rodale Books.

28. **Research also shows people working long hours are more likely to have a stroke and heart diseases:** Bazian, (2015, August 21). Working long hours 'increases stroke risk'. Retrieved from https://www.nhs.uk/news/neurology/working-long-hours-increases-stroke-risk/

29. **Our teachers often told us the legend of Sūn Jìng from the Han Dynasty. Sun Jing:** Fredericson, C. (2016, September 10). Chinese Idiom – Xuán Liáng Cì G – To Study Diligently and Tirelessly. Retrieved from https://bit.ly/2Y4Tn2z

30. **Professor John Pencavel from Stanford University found in his studies that employee output falls sharply after 50 working hours per week**: Pancavel, J. (2014). The Productivity of Working Hours. The Economic Journal, 125(589), 2052-2076. https://doi.org/10.1111/ecoj.12166

31. **We all have optimal periods when we are naturally more productive. Clinical psychologist Dr Michael Breus suggests in his groundbreaking book The Power of When**: Breus, M. (2016). The Power of When: Discover Your Chronotype--and the Best Time to Eat Lunch, Ask for a Raise, Have Sex, Write a Novel, Take Your Meds, and More. Little, Brown and Company

32. **Cal Newport has shared extensive research in his book Deep Work to show why the ability to concentrate and do deep work is one thing that will give information age workers huge advantage:** Newport, C. (2016). Deep Work: Rules for Focused Success in a Distracted World. Piatkus.

33. **Research supports this, walking in nature refreshes us:** Bratman,

G. Hamilton, P., Hahn, K., Daily, G., & Gross, J. (2015). Proceedings of the National Academy of Sciences. Nature experience reduces rumination and subgenual prefrontal cortex activation, 112(28), 8567-8572. https:// doi.org/10.1073/pnas.1510459112

34. **Increases our cognitive performance:** Berman, M. G., Jonides, J. & Kaplan, S. (2008). The cognitive benefits of interacting with nature (19), 1207-1212. https://www.naava.io/science/the-cognitive-benefits-of-interacting-with-nature

35. **As Seth Godin, author of Purple Cow says, In fact, many of us are stuck in a perpetual cycle of reacting and responding instead of innovating and initiating:** Godin, S. (2008, November 3). Reacting, Responding & Initiating. Retrieved from https://seths.blog/2008/11/reacting-respon/

36. **As Greg McKeown says in his book Essentialism, if you don't prioritise yourself, somebody else will:** McKeown, G. (2014, April 17). Essentialism: The Disciplined Pursuit of Less. Virgin Digital

37. **Researchers from the University of Leipzig have found that morning people are more proactive than evening types:** Randler, C. (2009). Journal of Applied Social Psychology. Proactive People Are Morning People, 39(12), 2787-2797. https://onlinelibrary.wiley.com/doi/abs/10.1111/j.1559-1816.2009.00549.x

38. **Meanwhile, morning is when we have the strongest willpower:** Lee, K. (2018, July 30). The Morning Routines Of The Most Successful People. Retrieved from https://www.fastcompany.com/3033652/the-morning-routines-of-the-most-successful-people

39. **According to the strength model, self-control is a finite resource: Hagger, M., Wood, C., Stiff, C., & Chatzisarantis, N. (2010). Psychological bulletin. Ego Depletion and the Strength Model of Self-Control:** A Meta-Analysis, 136(4), 495-525. https://www.researchgate.

net/publication/44689726_Ego_Depletion_and_the_ Strength_Model_ of_Self-Control_A_Meta-Analysis

40. **Bill Gates, the founder of Microsoft, spends one week alone, twice a year in a forest. He calls his ritual the "Think Week":** Muller, R. (2018, July 23). Bill Gates Spends Two Weeks Alone In the Forest Each Year. Here's Why. Retrieved from https://thriveglobal.com/stories/bill-gates-think-week/

41. **In a rare interview with Robert GuthStaff, a journalist from Wall Street Journal:** GuthStaff, R. (2005, March 28). In Secret Hideaway, Bill Gates Ponders Microsoft's Future. Retrieved from https://www.wsj.com/ articles/SB111196625830690477

42. **Research shows we lose up to 40% efficiency when we switch tasks regularly:** American Psychological Association (2006, March 20). Multitasking: Switching costs. Retrieved from https://www.apa.org/research/ action/multitask.aspx

43. **Neuroscience shows that our brain gains new insights from new environments** (Huffington, A. (2015). Thrive: The Third Metric to Redefining Success and Creating a Life of Well-Being, Wisdom, and Wonder. Harmony.

44. **In fact, research has shown that a moderate level of ambient noise created by places such as coffee shops improves our concentration and creativity:** Mehta, R., Zhu, R., & Cheema, A. (2012). Is Noise Always Bad? Exploring the Effects of Ambient Noise on Creative Cognition. Journal of Consumer Research, 39(4), 784-799.

45. **As John Maxwell says in his book, Make Today Count, "The secret of your success is determined by your daily agenda.":** Maxwell, J. (2008). Make Today Count: The Secret of Your Success Is Determined by Your Daily Agenda. Center Street.

Chapter 7

46. **Dr Emma Seppala, Standford University researcher and professor in the field of happiness, found that happiness was not the result of achievement; rather, it was the precursor of any sustainable success:** Seppala, E. Z(2017). The Happiness Track: How to Apply the Science of Happiness to Accelerate Your Success Paperback. Harperone.

47. **In her New York Times bestseller, Big Magic, Elizabeth Gilbert says there are many writers who want to write so they can become famous. To Gilbert, they are missing the point:** Gilbert, E. (2015). Big magic: Creative living beyond fear. London: Bloomsbury Publishing.

48. **However, research has shown that having fun reduces stress, improves our relationship, keeps us energetic, and increases more job satisfaction:** Rucker, M. (2016, December 11). Why You Need More Fun in Your Life, According to Science. Retrieved from https://michaelrucker.com/having-fun/why-you-need-more-fun- in-your-life/

49. **Dr Anthony Grant introduces the concept of fuzzy vision in his book, Coach Yourself:** Grant, A. & Greene, J. (2004). Coach Yourself: Make Real Changes in Your Life. Pearson Education UK.

50. **In her book, Bird by Bird, Anne Lamott, explains the best way to write is to start by filling a one-inch frame:** Lamott, A. (2007). Bird by Bird: Some Instructions on Writing and Life. (1st ed.). Anchor.

Praise for *Come Alive*

What a gift this book is! Yu Dan's story is captivating, honest and inspiring. There are so many practical life lessons rolled up into an easy-to-implement guide that would take most of us years to discover. This life-changing book made me laugh and cry, a must read for anyone searching for a simpler path to happiness.

Anneka Hunston
Customer Advocacy Leader APAC, Adobe

Is it possible to have both happiness and success? Yu Dan Shi has elegantly and empathetically written a book that leads you on a pathway to a life with meaning, purpose, and joy. It inspires from the first page with stories and insights, through to the incredibly practical exercises that you can put into action for yourself. This book is a breath of fresh air in an age of busyness and over-achievement.

Kirryn Zerna
Social Brand & Influence Expert

Come Alive is brilliantly written shining the light on every aspect of our life. It challenges but gently guides the reader to where they need to go. Yu Dan's authenticity takes you on a journey of self-discovery at your own pace. It's a must read for anyone who is over the "How-to" self-help books.

Patricia Theodor
Financial Services Consultant, OnePath, ANZ Bank

When I finish a book and immediately feel the need to read it again the impact is evident. While stemming from different backgrounds, so much of Yu Dan's narrative was inherently relatable. Yu Dan's journey and implementable, practical techniques for creating positive change are life-changing for anyone questioning or 'feeling stuck' at any stage along their professional journey.

Nicole Gemmell
Founder of Mave Agency, PR & Communications Expert

Yu Dan's training is the best personal development program I have ever attended! I entered the program feeling disengaged and disenchanted with my job, and it was impacting the rest of my life in a negative way. I left the program feeling energised. The program has inspired me to do things in my daily life differently and explore opportunities that I never thought were possible. For anyone needing a new lease on life this program is for you.

Kacie Serls
Head of Customer Service, Reprise

Attending Yu Dan's program has been a game changer for me. Yu Dan's inspirational journey and practical techniques are a rare combination and have helped me solve the crux of my career development dilemma. I have gained so much clarity and strength from her workshops and coaching sessions that I am finally living the life that I only dare to dream.

Bonnie Xi
Business Coach, Cross-Border Brand Strategist

I have attended a number of courses, seminars, and workshops over the years. Yu Dan's training is one of the best. Using extensive research alongside her own vulnerability, she takes participants on a journey of self-awareness and discovery beautifully and empathetically. The program has given the direction, clarity, purpose and renewed energy I needed for my business and myself. I am back in flow with absolute clarity. It's one of the best things I have done in my life.

Charlie Pidcock
Sales Coach, Trainer and Mentor

ABOUT THE AUTHOR

Yu Dan Shi is a coach, mentor, speaker and author with more than 20 years' experience of bringing out the best in people. After hitting rock bottom in 2008 while working as an executive for a global technology company, Yu Dan was compelled to search for more meaningful ways to work and live.

Today, Yu Dan combines her expertise in business, psychology and peak performance to help high-achieving professionals, executives and entrepreneurs reach their true potential and live a more fulfilled life.

Before establishing her practice, Yu Dan held senior leadership roles within various Fortune 100 companies. She was the Asia Pacific Director of Strategy at Adobe, and Chief Marketing Officer at Lenovo and Cisco in Australia and New Zealand.

Yu Dan has a Master of Coaching Psychology from the University of Sydney. Yu Dan was born in Shanghai, China, and has resided in Sydney, Australia, since 1997.

www.yudanshi.com

www.ingramcontent.com/pod-product-compliance
Lightning Source LLC
Chambersburg PA
CBHW062059290426
44110CB00022B/2643